{BIRDS OF A FEATHER}

Wildfowl Carving in Southeast Louisiana

THE HISTORIC NEW ORLEANS COLLECTION

PART 1

OCTOBER 23, 2007–JANUARY 7, 2008

PART 2

JANUARY 15–APRIL 20, 2008

LOUISIANA'S POSITION ON THE MISSISSIPPI FLYWAY has made duck hunting a part of our culture since time immemorial. Over time, as hunters became more numerous and ducks less so, human ingenuity was put to the test. The advent of the wooden duck decoy not only bettered the odds for the hunter but also marked the birth of an art form.

Early decoys, while utilitarian, nonetheless were artistic expressions from the hands of skilled carvers. As molded plastic decoys replaced wooden working decoys, the art form evolved. Decoys migrated from the marshes to the mantels of collectors' homes.

The Historic New Orleans Collection is pleased to present what we believe to be the most comprehensive exhibition of southeast Louisiana decoys ever mounted. The works on display span more than a century; represent the finest examples of the region's distinct carving traditions; and, in many cases, demonstrate the persistence of the carver's art through several generations of a single family.

Every successful exhibition is a collaborative effort. *Birds of a Feather* benefited from the generosity of its advisory committee, whose members volunteered their time, their expertise, and their important holdings to the show.

The Historic New Orleans Collection remains dedicated to the public presentation of significant aspects of our history, culture, and art. Many of the most important examples of Louisiana decoys are, at present, privately held. Partnership with numerous private collectors has permitted us to realize the expansive vision of *Birds of a Feather.*

Charles Snyder
President, Board of Directors
The Historic New Orleans Collection

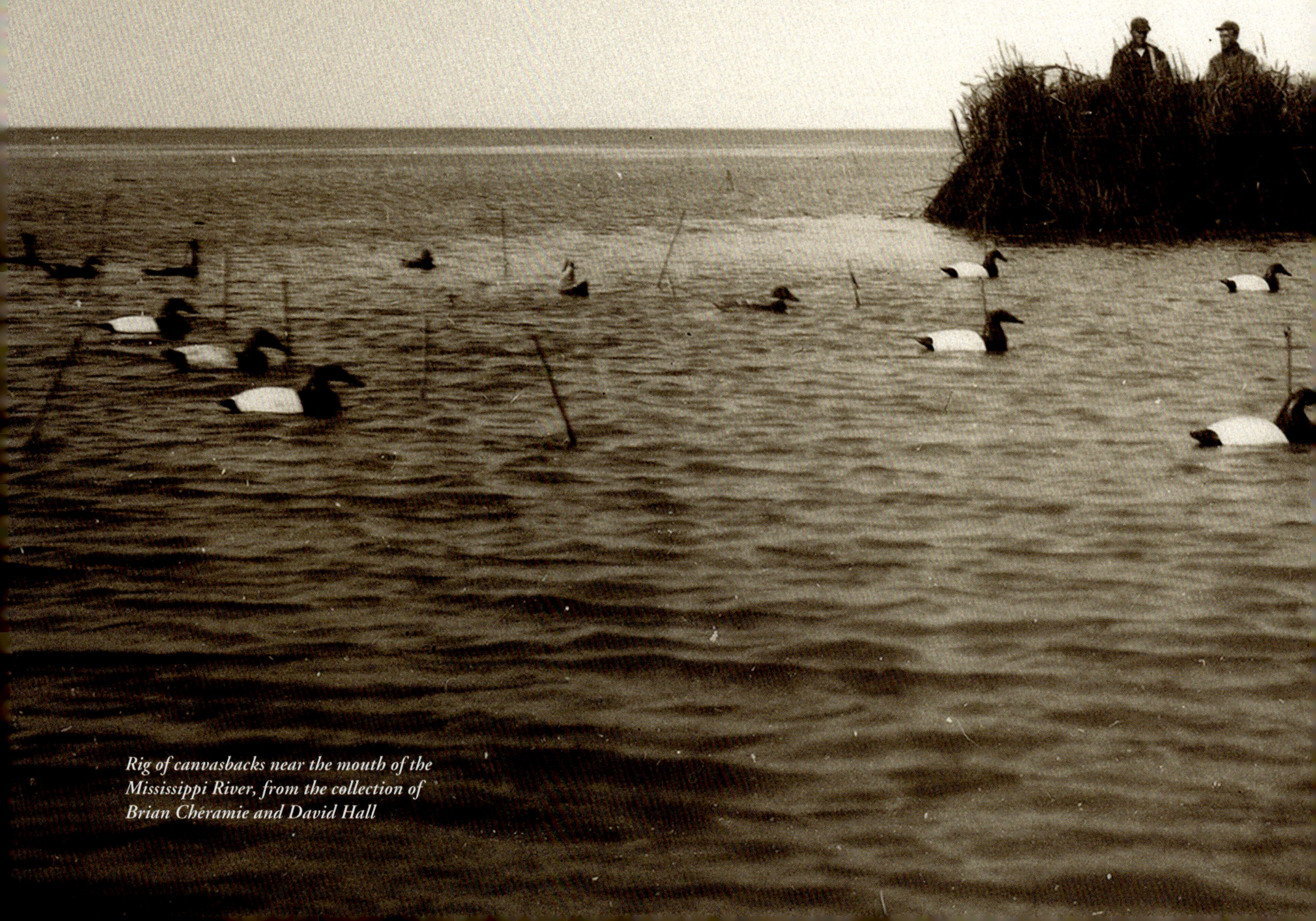

Rig of canvasbacks near the mouth of the Mississippi River, from the collection of Brian Chéramie and David Hall

AT TIMES THE POPULATION OF LOUISIANA DECOYS seems to exceed that of the wild ducks (and collectors) they attract. Given the amplitude of options, assembling a decoy exhibition demands difficult choices. The examples selected for Part 1 of *Birds of a Feather* celebrate those early carvers who helped establish the regional styles of southeast Louisiana. Those selected for Part 2 showcase the talents of skilled decorative carvers, the inheritors of the working decoy tradition.

It has been 15 years since the New Orleans area has seen an exhibition focused on Louisiana decoys, their carvers, and their habitats. So long as decoy carving remains a living art, periodic assessments of the Pelican State's carving traditions are invaluable. Though *Birds of a Feather* is hardly the final word on the state of decoy carving in Louisiana, we are proud to offer a comprehensive review of this ever-evolving art form.

Robert C. Baird
Committee Chair
Brian Cheramie
William Hanemann
Richard Stephens
John F. White
Birds of a Feather Advisory Committee

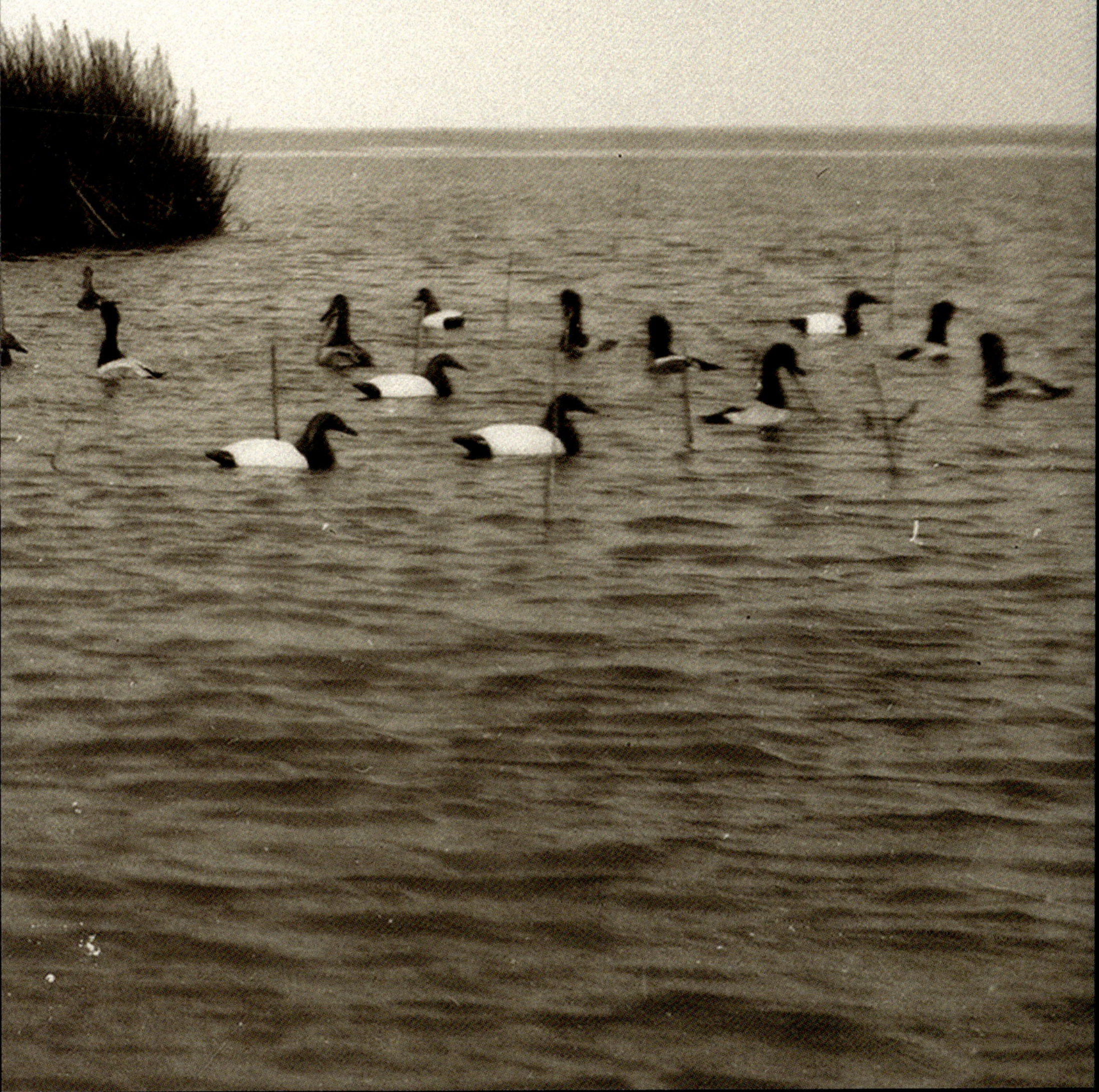

{CONTENTS}

An Introduction to the Southeast Louisiana Carving Tradition

On the most basic level, a decoy is a block of wood—simply (if often expertly) shaped and decorated to deceive. But whether considered as discrete objects or transmitters of a larger folkloric tradition, decoys transcend their material essence. They offer paths to exploring Louisiana's unique individuals, communities, and cultures. Observed over time, their production, use, and status describe changes in people and places.

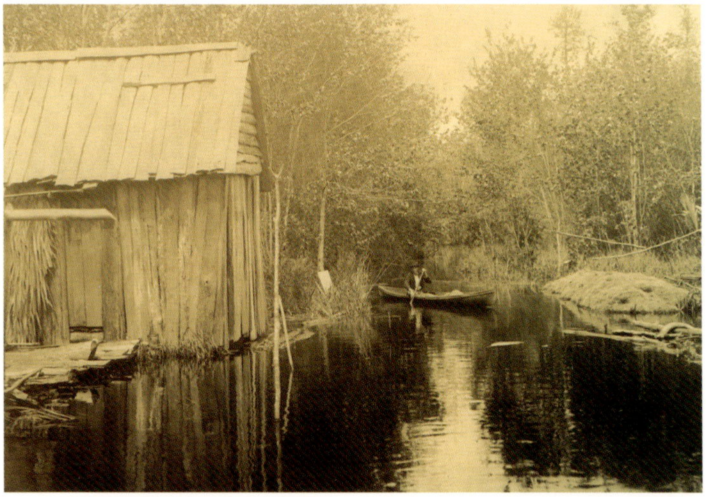

Pirogue on the bayou (1974.25.31.55)

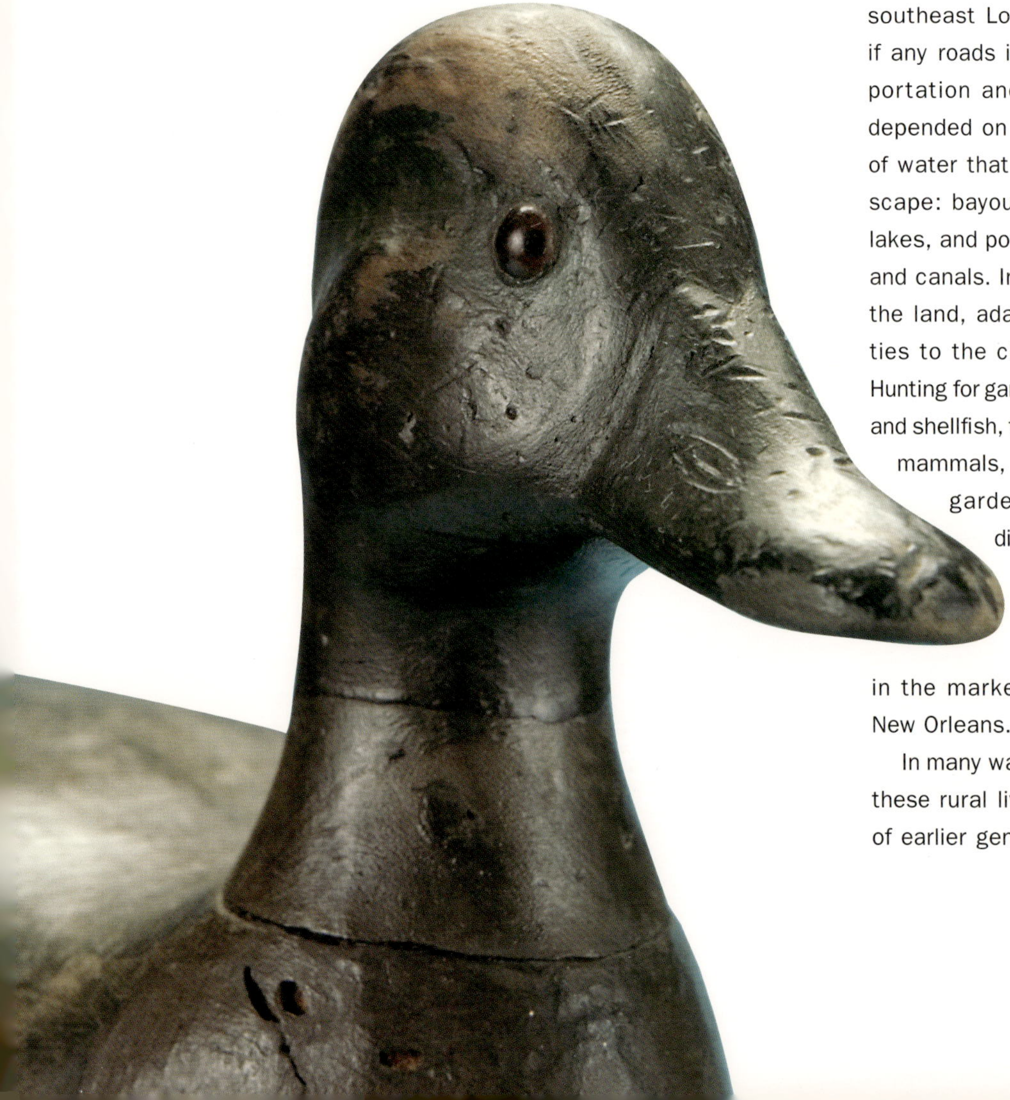

IN THE 19TH CENTURY, decoys were one of many tools employed by inhabitants of remote, marshy southeast Louisiana. With few if any roads in the area, transportation and communication depended on the intricate web of water that defined the landscape: bayous; tidal marshes, lakes, and ponds; distributaries and canals. Individuals lived off the land, adapting their activities to the changing seasons. Hunting for game, catching finfish and shellfish, trapping furbearing mammals, and tending small garden plots provided dietary variety—and, in some cases, also provided foodstuffs to sell in the markets in and around New Orleans.

In many ways, the patterns of these rural lives recalled those of earlier generations of Native Americans. Some carvers, like Laurent Verdin Sr. of Houma, could in fact claim Native American ancestry. Others, like Mitchel Lafrance, came from African American or Afro-Creole wetlands communities. Still others, like Clovis "Cadice" Vizier, settled among the Cajuns whose forebears made their way to Louisiana after being expelled from Nova Scotia in the mid-18th century. And in St. Bernard Parish, carvers like Domingo Campo belonged to the Isleño community, established during Louisiana's Spanish colonial era by immigrants from the Canary Islands.

Not all southeast Louisiana carvers were isolated rural folk. A number of mid-20th-century decoy makers, like Jim Mossmeier, were New Orleans businessmen with a passion for woodworking and an appreciation for hunting with self-fabricated

{ GREEN-WINGED TEAL DRAKE }
by Nicole Vidacovich

decoys. Some carvers, especially in communities downriver from New Orleans, produced decoys as a sideline, making their primary living as farmers or skilled craftsmen: carpenters, bricklayers, plasterers. But whether the decoys came from the banks of the Mississippi River; the bayous Terrebonne, Lafourche, Gauche, or Barataria; or the shores of lakes Pontchartrain, Borgne, or Des Allemands, their purpose was to serve the hunter in the quest for game birds.

Each of North America's four principal migratory flyways (Atlantic, Mississippi, Central, and Pacific) boasts a tradition of waterfowl and game bird carving. The carvers of the Atlantic flyway were the first to garner widespread attention; their decoys were celebrated for their aesthetic qualities in the early years of the 20th century. Similar recognition was long denied Louisiana carvers. Although a few exhibited decoys in out-of-state competitions, the vast majority remained as unknown, outside Louisiana, as the landscape they inhabited.

Following the Second World War, a number of independent factors transformed the practice of decoy carving in southeast Louisiana. New roads, improved telecommunications, and the gradual attrition of non-English-speaking residents combined to make rural communities less isolated. And the introduction of mass-manufactured decoys made it impractical for the cottage-industry carver to compete economically. Although some carvers resisted change, others embraced it. One, Robert Couret, invented a duplicating lathe that permitted large-scale manufacture of wooden decoys. Decorated with stenciled markings applied with a spraygun, Couret's birds were marketed under the brand "Lifelike Lures."

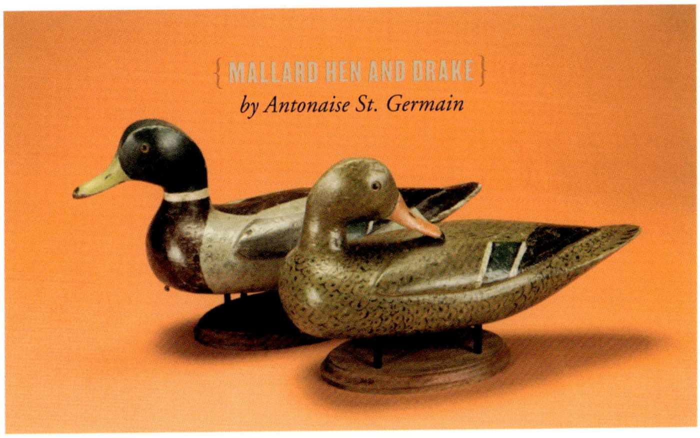

{MALLARD HEN AND DRAKE}
by Antonaise St. Germain

The "opening up" of southeast Louisiana had the ironic effect of making the area's carvers better known to a larger audience—national as well as local—even as it diminished the traditional basis for their work. The oil and gas industries brought regular rather than seasonally cyclical employment to the area. Though carvers continued to carve, and to pass the tradition along to succeeding generations of craftsmen, "working birds" were made for personal use or for a select group of clients and friends. In recent decades, the demand for antique decoys—a finite quantity—has run parallel, among collectors, with the demand for decorative birds.

Although it is impossible to fix a specific year as a watershed, by 1960 decorative decoys had eclipsed functional decoys across southeast Louisiana. The purpose of a decoy was no longer to attract birds within gunshot range, but to exemplify the artist's dexterity in carving and painting. Though aesthetic concerns had occasionally motivated members of the older generation of carvers, decorative decoys became the principal form of expression for the younger generation. National and international competitions were soon attracting, and honoring, Louisiana carvers. Among the regional artists to win top awards are Tan Brunet, Jett Brunet, and Jimmie Vizier, featured in Part 2 of *Birds of a Feather.*

John H. Lawrence
Director of Museum Programs

Erin Greenwald
Exhibitions Editor

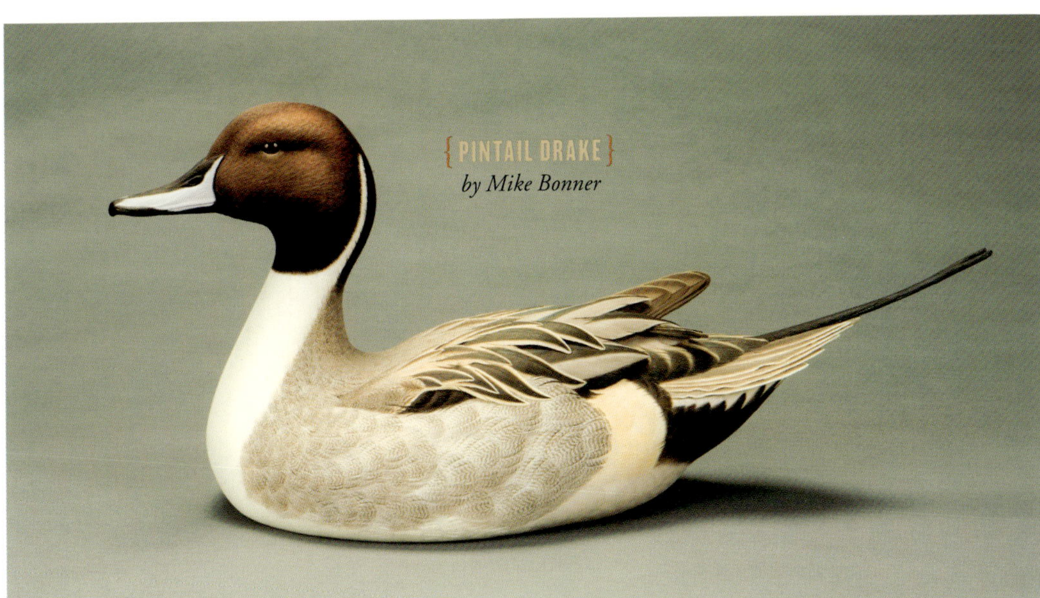

{PINTAIL DRAKE}
by Mike Bonner

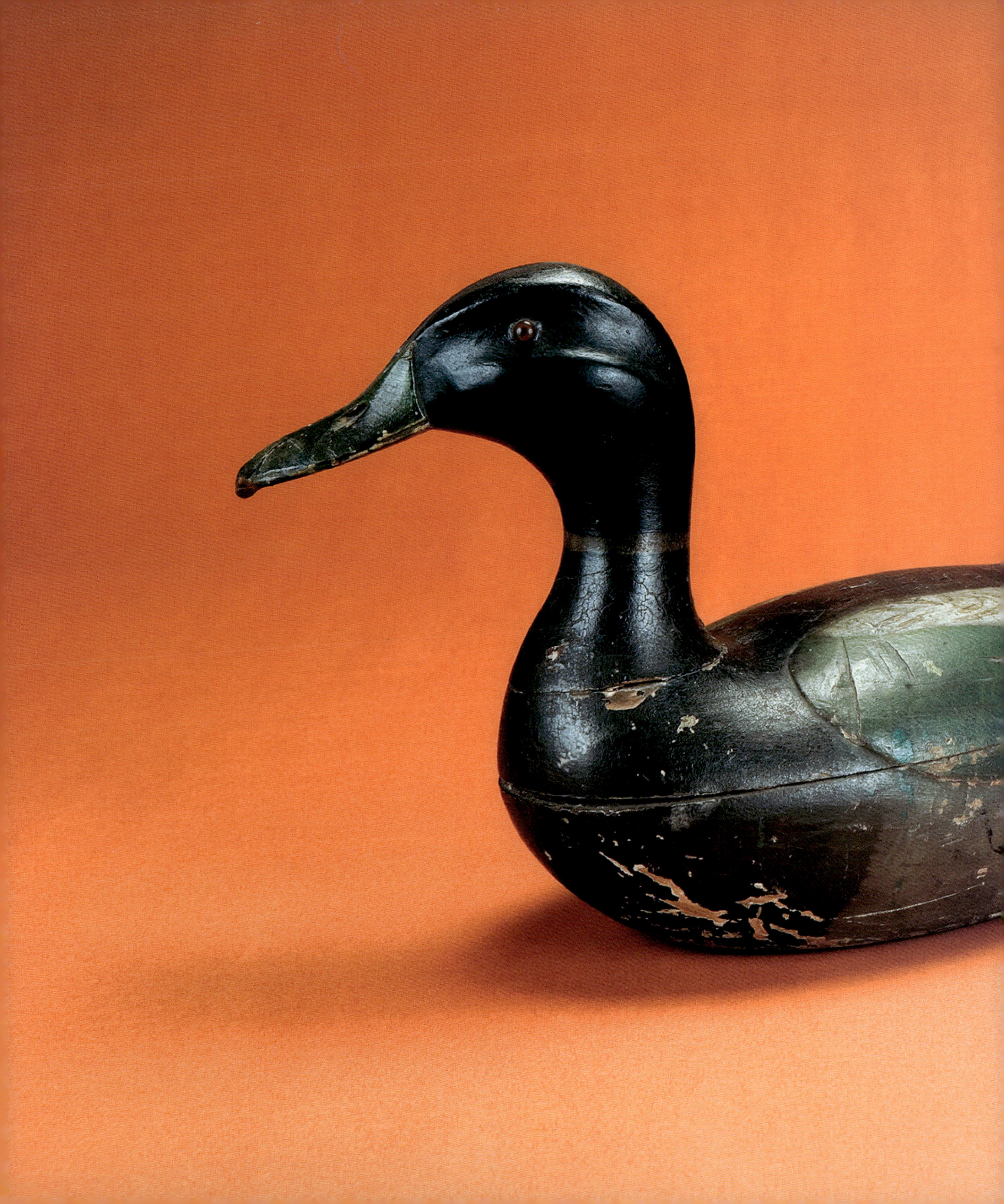

{ **MALLARD DRAKE** }
by an unknown carver

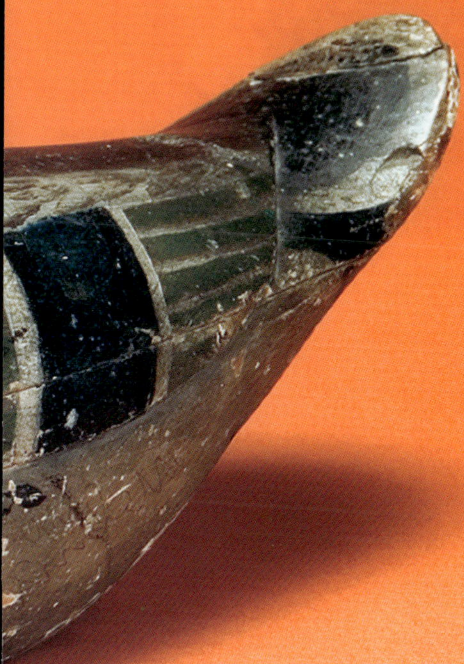

{ BIRDS OF A FEATHER }

Wildfowl Carving in Southeast Louisiana

THE HISTORIC NEW ORLEANS COLLECTION

This two-part exhibition offers an introduction to the art and history of wildfowl carving in southeast Louisiana. PART 1: EARLY WORKING DECOYS profiles notable carvers and examines the distinctive carving styles associated with seven geographic regions. PART 2: CONTEMPORARY CARVINGS traces the evolution of wildfowl carving from folk art to fine art, introducing some of today's most celebrated decorative carvers.

{ THE SPECIES }

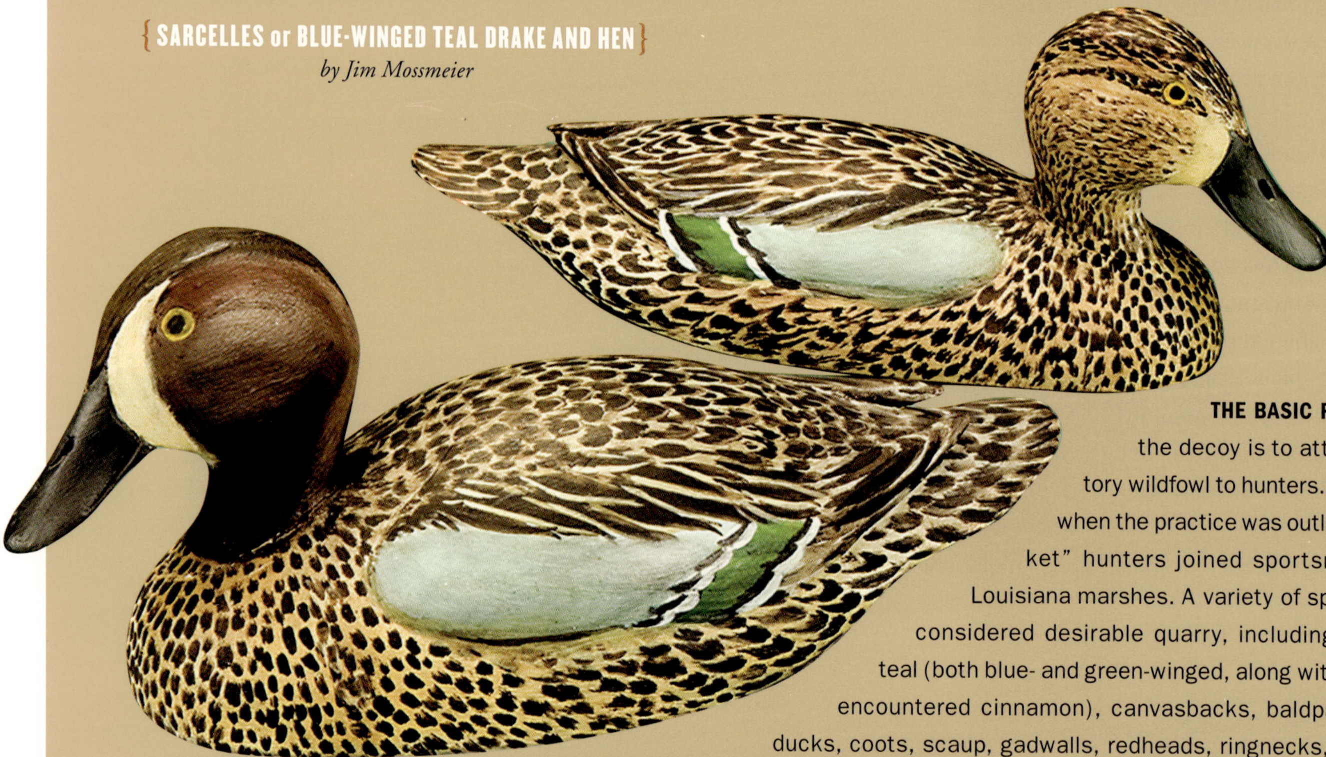

{ SARCELLES or BLUE-WINGED TEAL DRAKE AND HEN }
by Jim Mossmeier

THE BASIC FUNCTION of the decoy is to attract migratory wildfowl to hunters. Until 1900, when the practice was outlawed, "market" hunters joined sportsmen in the Louisiana marshes. A variety of species were considered desirable quarry, including mallards, teal (both blue- and green-winged, along with the rarely encountered cinnamon), canvasbacks, baldpates, wood ducks, coots, scaup, gadwalls, redheads, ringnecks, shovelers, hooded mergansers, pintails, and buffleheads.

Louisiana hunters had colorful local names for these birds, often derived from French terms. Mallards were known as French ducks or *canards français;* teal were sometimes called *sarcelles;* and canvasbacks might be referred to as *canards chevaux* (or horse ducks) due to the slope of their heads. Baldpates were widgeons, *zin-zins* or *zan-zans;* wood ducks were *branchiers* (for their habit of roosting in trees) or squealers; coots were *poules d'eau* (water chickens); scaup were *dos gris* (gray backs) or blue bills; and gadwalls might be called gray ducks or *canards gris.* Because of the sound their wings made while flying, redheads were called *violons* (violins). Ringnecks were black ducks and, locally, shovelers were spoonbills. The bufflehead, although rarely spotted in the region, earned the sobriquet butterball for its rounded and compressed body. Hooded mergansers were identified as *becs scie* (or saw bills), while Louisiana hunters might refer to pintails as sprig-tails, long-necked ducks, or *pian queues* (straw tails).

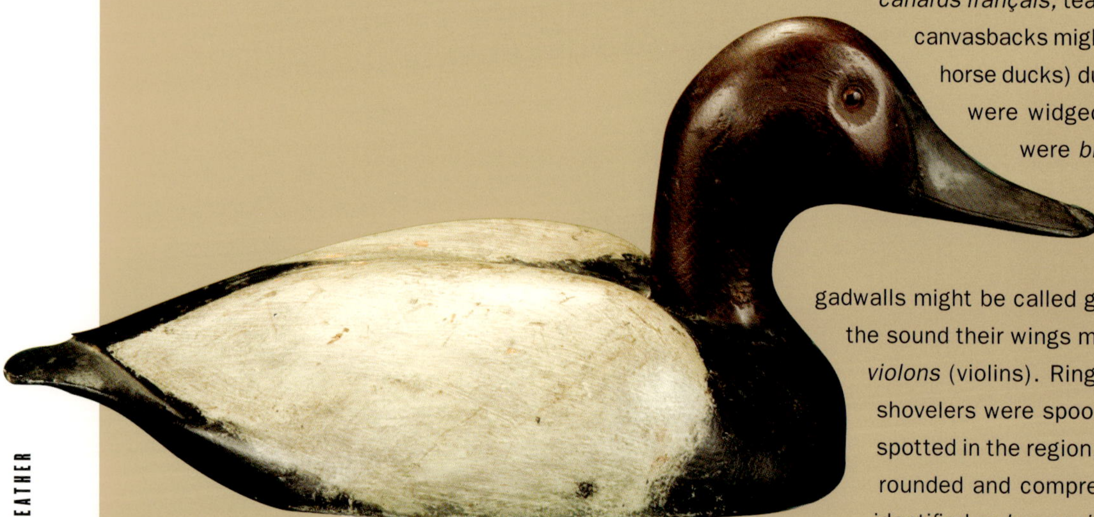

{ CANARD CHEVAL or CANVASBACK }
by Al Beyl

{DECOY POSES}

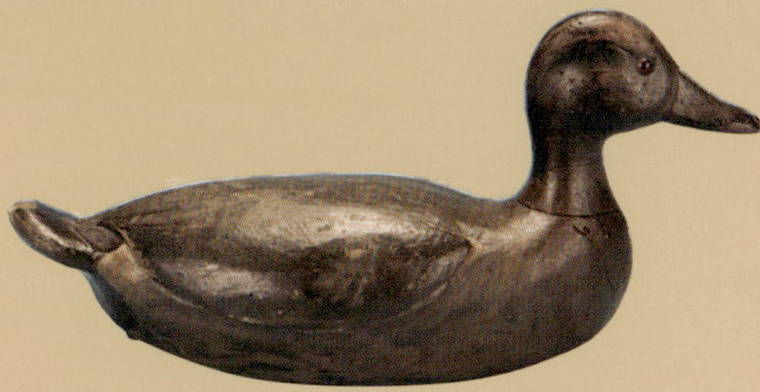

{GUNNER}
Green-winged teal drake by Nicole Vidacovich

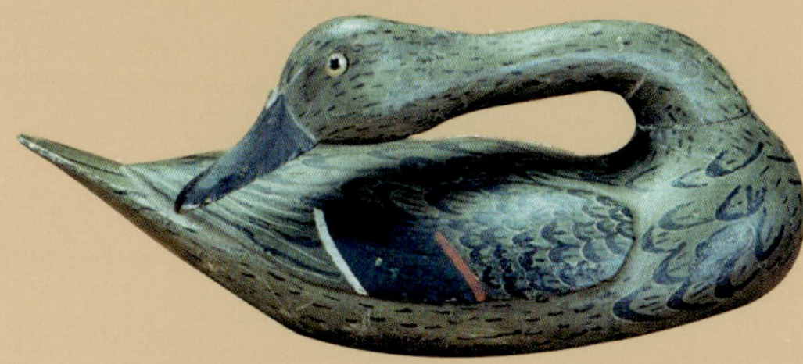

{PREENER}
Pintail hen by Mitchel Lafrance, Charles Numa Joefrau, and George Frederick Jr.

NOT ALL DECOYS resemble the "shooting gallery" profile *(gunner)* of a duck floating on water. Carvers mimicked a range of activities and habits in order to give a rig of decoys a more natural flock-like appearance. Among the typical poses are *sippers* (with the head thrown back slightly to replicate a duck's swallowing motion); *preeners* (with the bird's head turned to the rear and the bill grooming the feathers); *swimmers* (with the head and tail turned slightly to one side); and *minnow chasers* (with the neck extended and the bill low to the water, as if in pursuit of small fish). Birds were also presented "at rest" in different ways. One of the most popular positions shows the neck retracted, with the head seemingly attached to the body. Another at rest variation is the *tucked* position, which resembles preening but presents the neck flatter on the back and the bill more deeply buried in the feathers. Perhaps most unusual of all is the *tip-up*, a half-decoy that simulated the appearance of a duck feeding underwater. Only the back half of the body and the tail are visible in this pose. Another type of decoy, a *confidence decoy*, represented non-hunted species, thereby enhancing the "natural" feel of the setting. Wading birds such as herons and egrets were often chosen as confidence decoys.

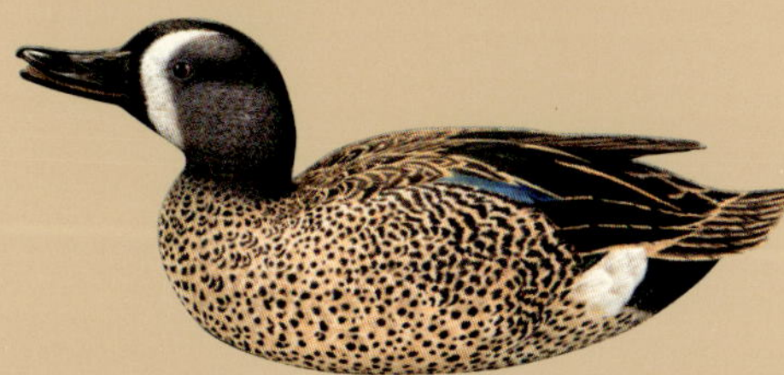

{SIPPER}
Blue-winged teal drake by Tan Brunet

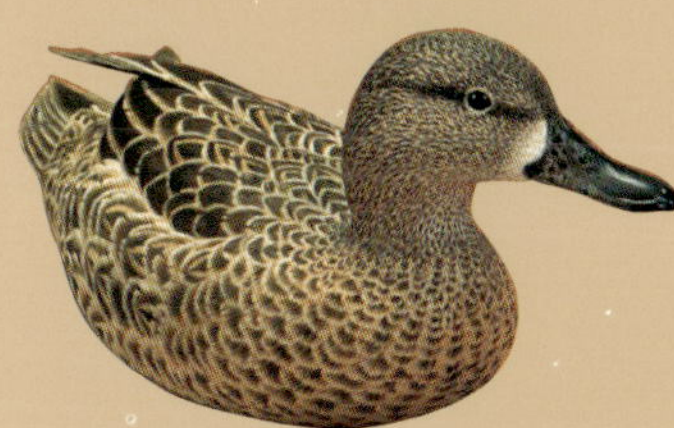

{SWIMMER}
Blue-winged teal hen by Tan Brunet

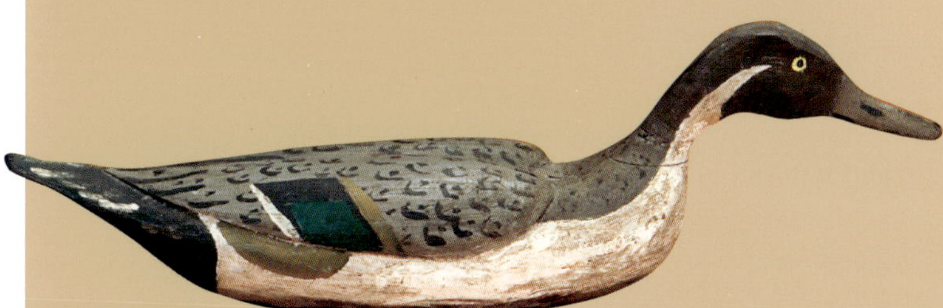

{MINNOW CHASER}
Pintail drake by Odee Vizier

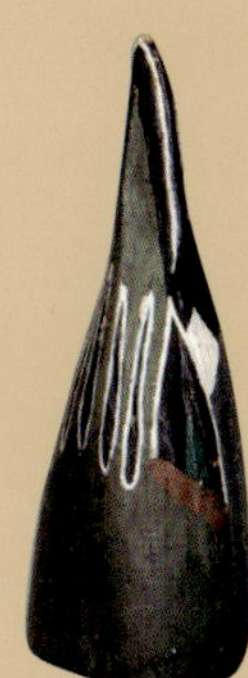

{TIP-UP}
Tip-up pintail by Nicole Vidacovich

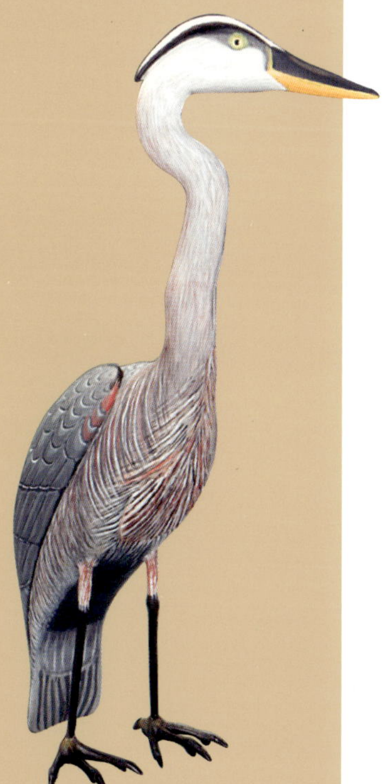

{CONFIDENCE DECOY}
Blue heron by Laurent Verdin Jr.

{ CARVER INGENUITY }

THROUGH THE YEARS carvers have made imaginative use of the resources at hand. Although carving methods, tools, and materials have changed, ingenuity has remained a constant.

The question of decoy eyes has prompted particularly creative responses. While Laurent Verdin Sr. fashioned eyes out of bits of brown glass taken from New Orleans-brewed Jax beer bottles, other carvers requisitioned everyday household objects such as hatpins and tacks—or chose to carve the eyes rather than use supplementary materials. A handful of early carvers, including Nicole Vidacovich, used high-quality (and high-priced) taxidermy eyes, a practice now commonplace in contemporary carving circles.

Over the years, the decoy's painted finish has evolved both physically and philosophically. The paint on early working birds was meant to be convincing—but not, necessarily, ornithologically precise. Today's decorative carver adheres to exacting standards of feather count and shape and attempts to match the hue and iridescence of a species' plumage, using application tools that range from red-sable paintbrushes to airbrushes.

If painting techniques have grown increasingly sophisticated, so too have carving methods. Where once a hatchet or broadaxe was used to hew a carving block to shape, a modern carver would be more likely to employ an electric bandsaw. Knives, a perennial staple of the carver's kit, have evolved as well—from the pocket knife or drawknife of earlier days to highly specialized tools made specifically for carving. Nontraditional tools and innovative techniques permit decorative carvers to achieve the exceptional level of detail demanded by competitions like the annual Ward World Championship. From red-hot ice picks used as makeshift branding irons, to cosmetic bronzing powders that lend feathers their sheen, contemporary carvers employ a battery of tools—both homemade and high-tech—in their efforts to make their art as lifelike as possible.

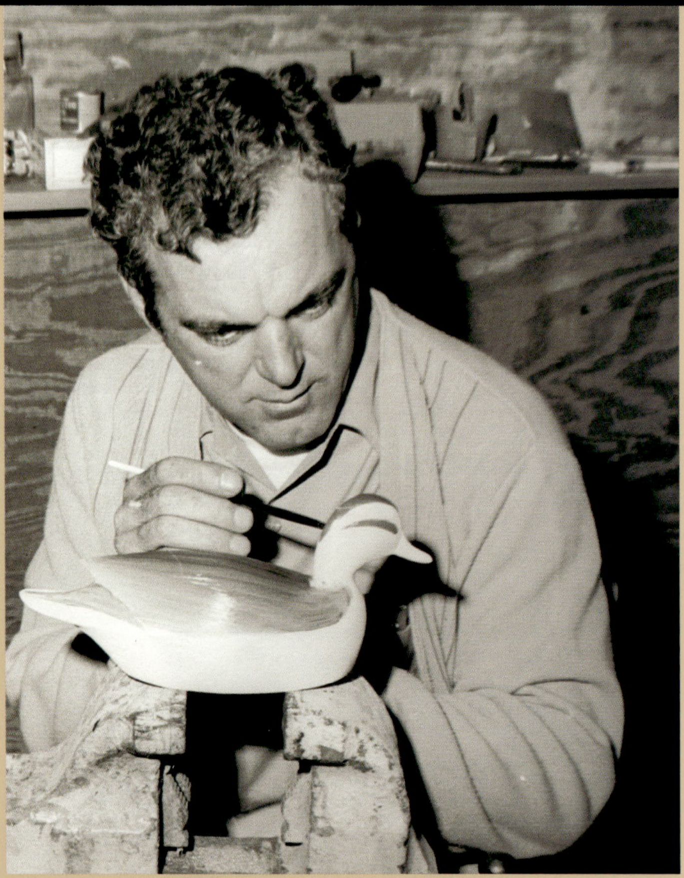

Jimmie Vizier, from the collection of Brian Cheramie and David Hall

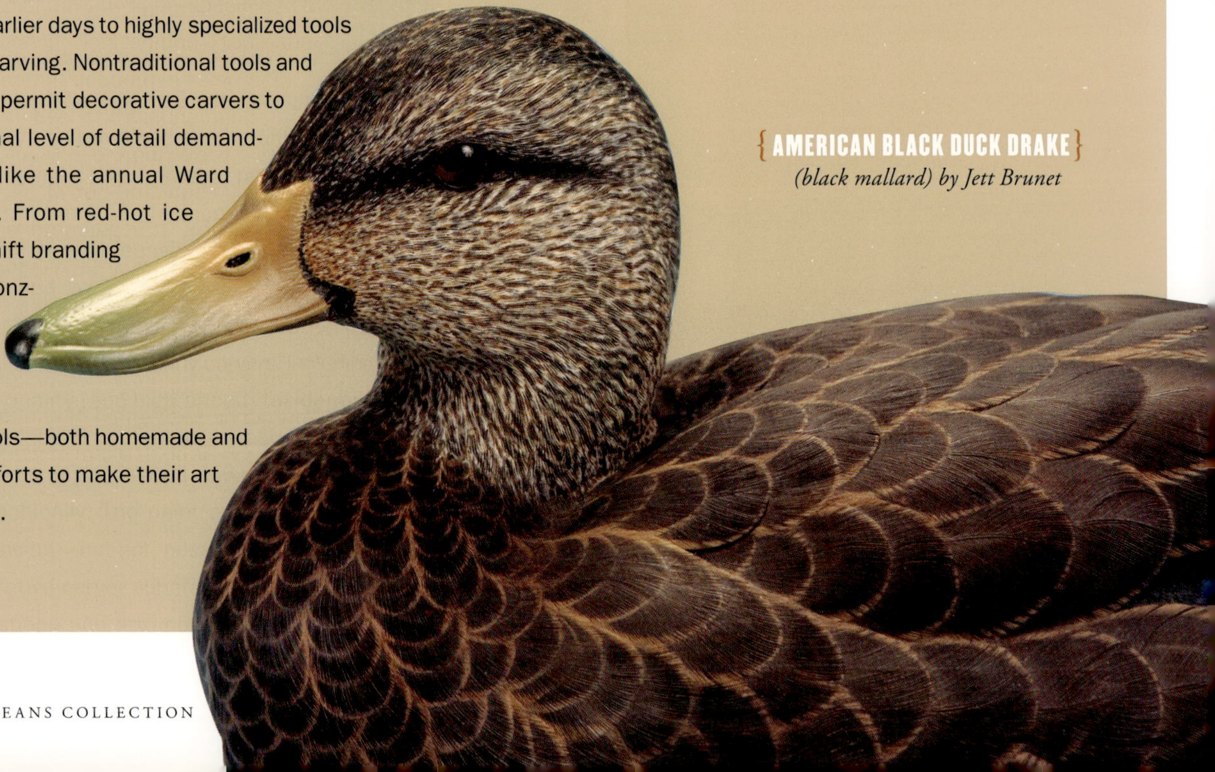

{ **AMERICAN BLACK DUCK DRAKE** }
(black mallard) by Jett Brunet

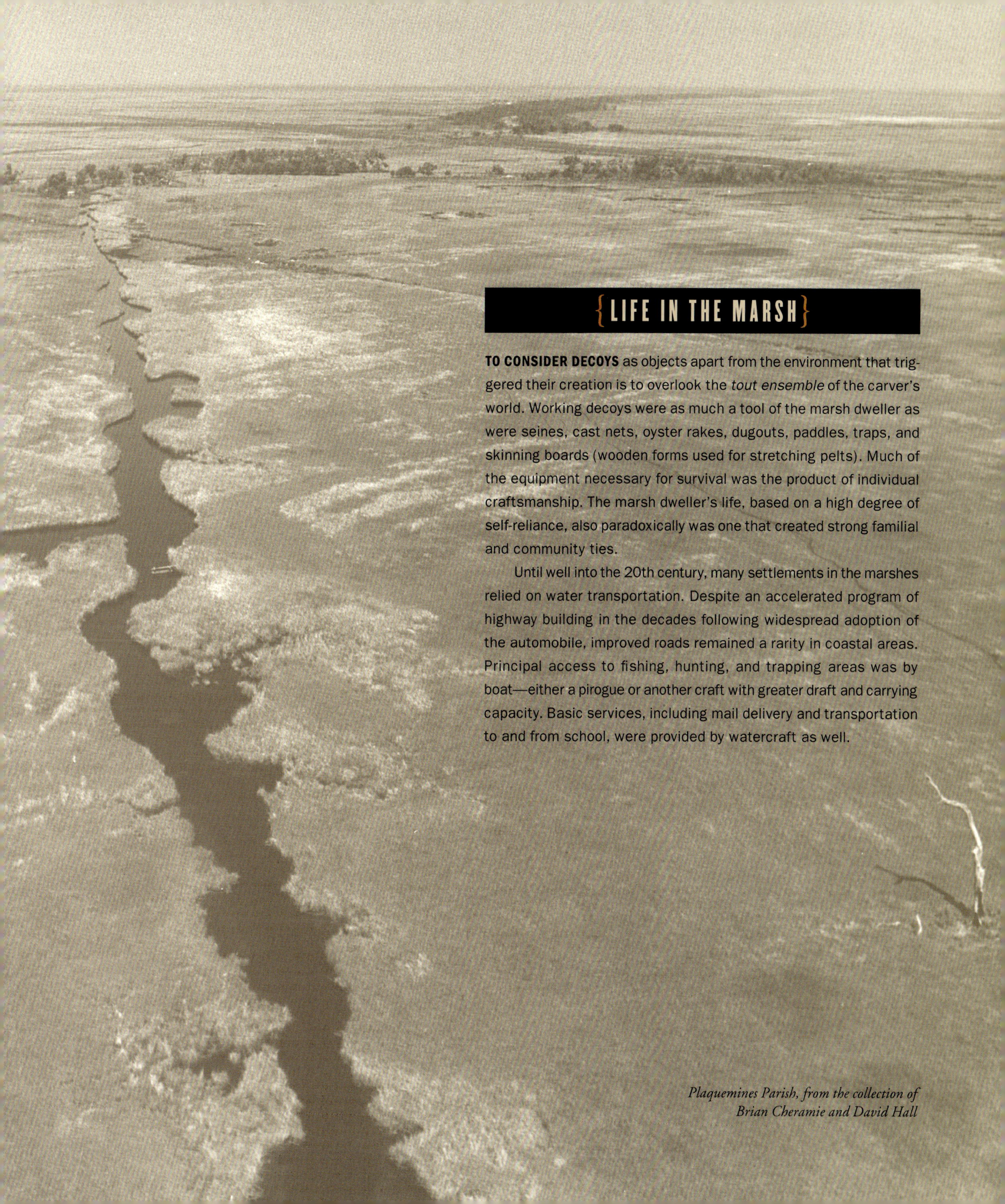

LIFE IN THE MARSH

TO CONSIDER DECOYS as objects apart from the environment that triggered their creation is to overlook the *tout ensemble* of the carver's world. Working decoys were as much a tool of the marsh dweller as were seines, cast nets, oyster rakes, dugouts, paddles, traps, and skinning boards (wooden forms used for stretching pelts). Much of the equipment necessary for survival was the product of individual craftsmanship. The marsh dweller's life, based on a high degree of self-reliance, also paradoxically was one that created strong familial and community ties.

Until well into the 20th century, many settlements in the marshes relied on water transportation. Despite an accelerated program of highway building in the decades following widespread adoption of the automobile, improved roads remained a rarity in coastal areas. Principal access to fishing, hunting, and trapping areas was by boat—either a pirogue or another craft with greater draft and carrying capacity. Basic services, including mail delivery and transportation to and from school, were provided by watercraft as well.

Plaquemines Parish, from the collection of Brian Cheramie and David Hall

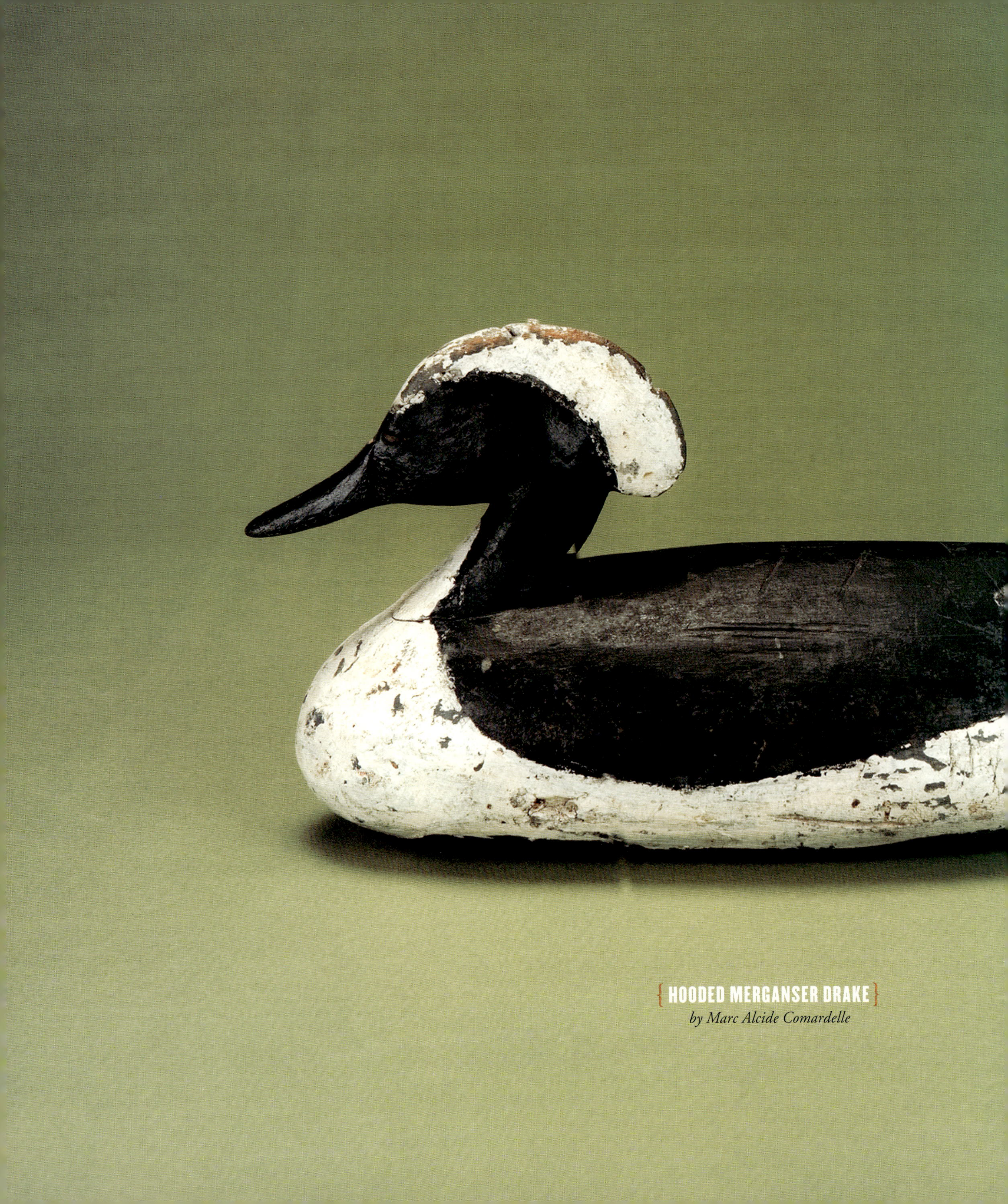

{ HOODED MERGANSER DRAKE }

by Marc Alcide Comardelle

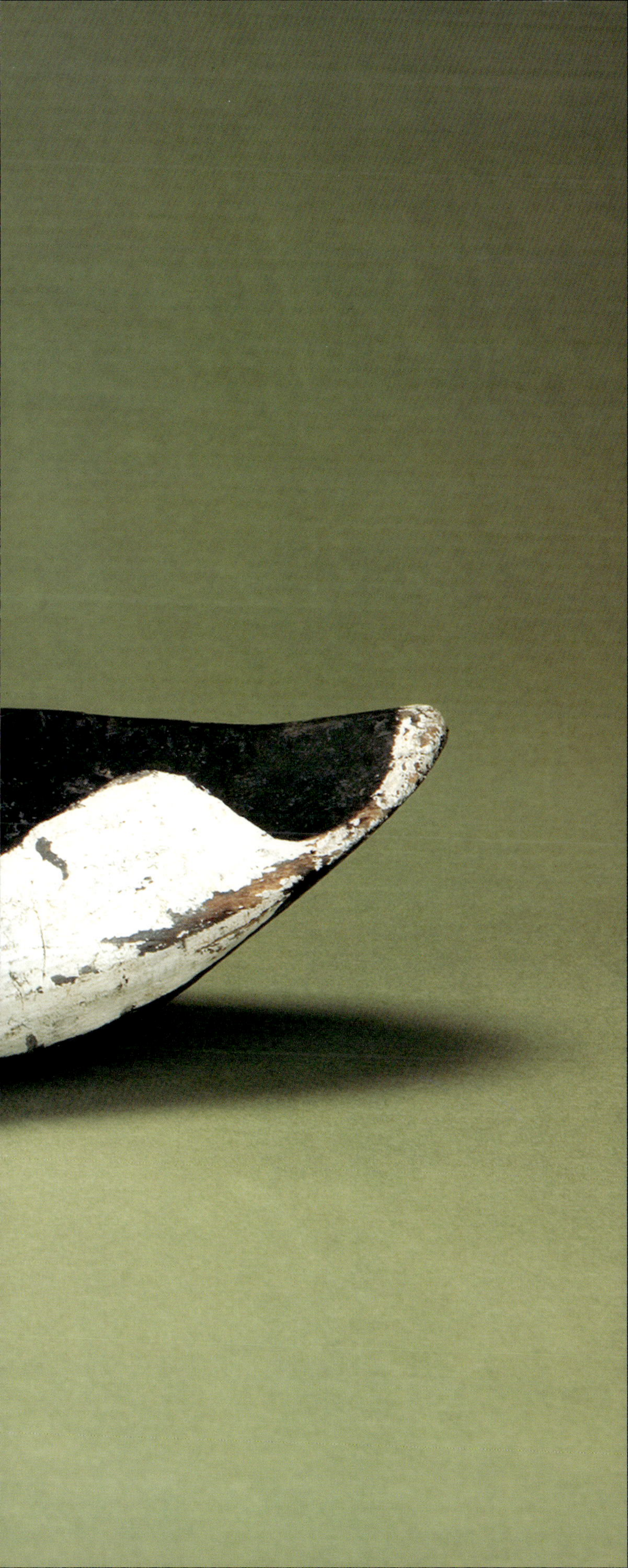

{BIRDS OF A FEATHER}

Wildfowl Carving in Southeast Louisiana

PART 1

EARLY WORKING DECOYS

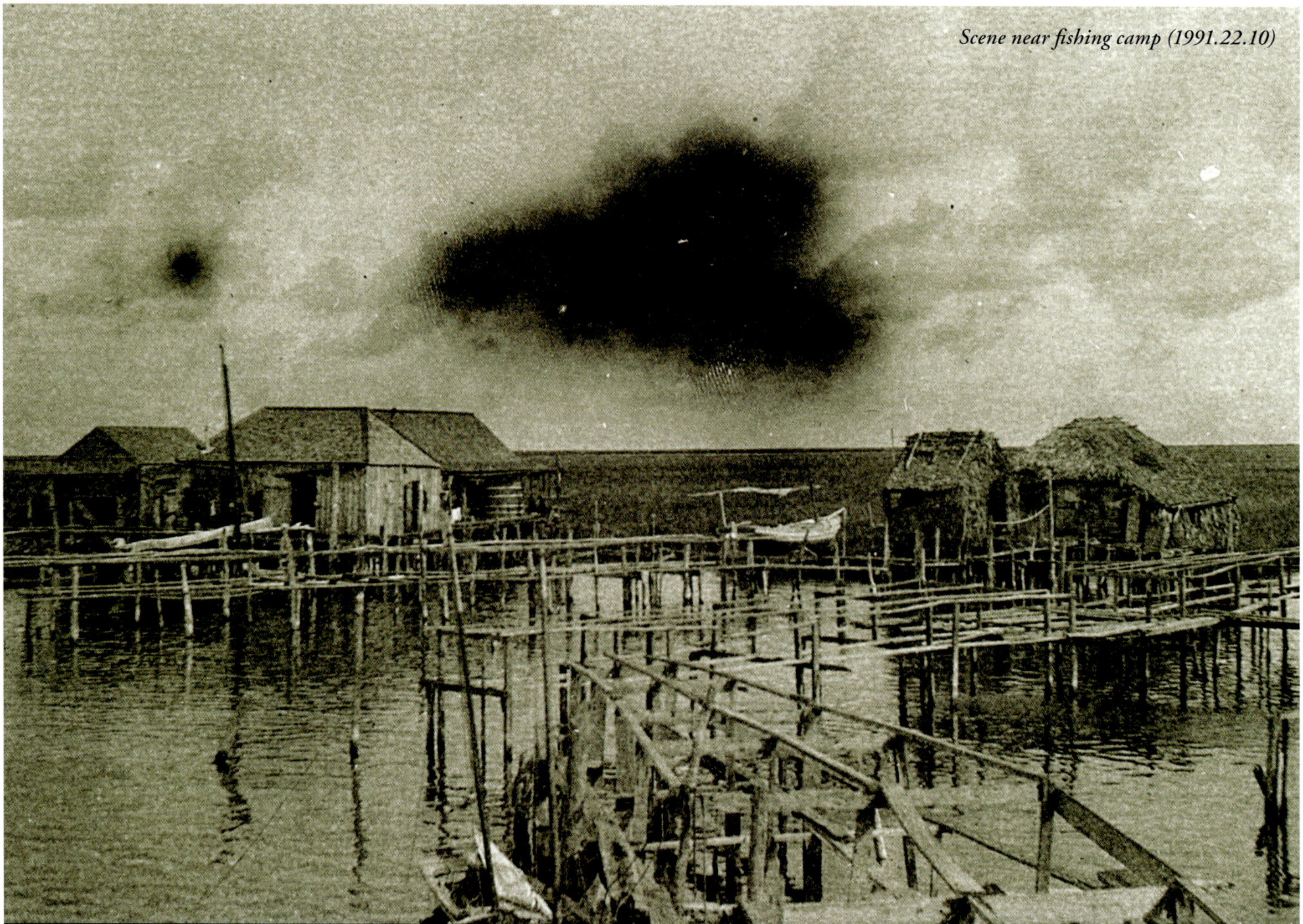

Scene near fishing camp (1991.22.10)

{HOUMA AND BAYOU TERREBONNE}

SOME SIXTY MILES WEST of New Orleans, the town of Houma—named for the area's early Native American inhabitants—is traversed by seven bayous. The longest of these, Bayou Terrebonne, passes through the coastal marsh communities of Montegut, Chauvin, and Cocodrie on its way to Terrebonne Bay, an arm of the Gulf of Mexico. Cocodrie once was home to a traditional shrimp preserving operation, with shrimp laid on elevated wooden platforms to dry in the sun. Settlers from the Philippines were the backbone of this enterprise, which was founded in the 19th century. Today, oil, gas, and seafood are the principal industries of the area, which also lures sport fishermen and hunters.

Some of the carvers along Bayou Terrebonne are of Native American ancestry. Over many generations, members of these communities have intermarried with other ethnic groups, creating a rich heritage fed by multiple traditions.

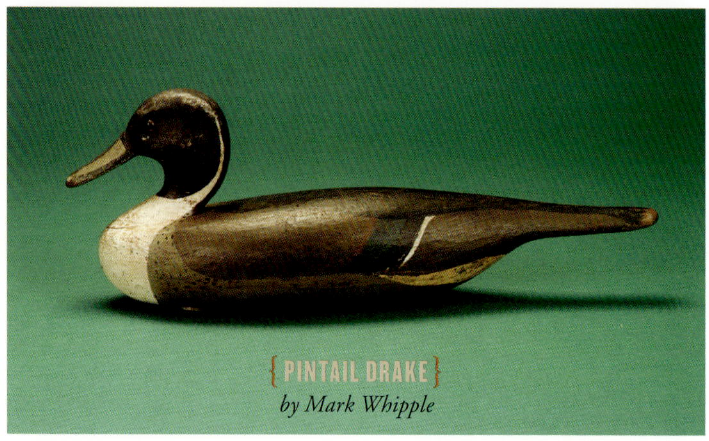

{PINTAIL DRAKE}
by Mark Whipple

Carvers of note from the area include **Walton Champagne, Laurent Verdin Sr.**, and **Mark Whipple.**

{LAURENT VERDIN SR.}

LAURENT VERDIN SR. (1909–1991) of Crooked Bayou Blue has frequently been cited as one of the last working-decoy carvers in southeast Louisiana. Despite failing eyesight and poor health in his later years, Verdin maintained a lifelong dedication to the production of functional decoys. A prolific carver, he was capable of producing more than one thousand decoys per year. His decoys were usually folk-art-inspired renderings of pintail, teal, and mallard ducks, but he also produced the occasional confidence decoy. Unlike most other carvers, Verdin did not select and rough out his own carving blocks. Instead, he relied almost exclusively on blocks of cypress root and tupelo gum brought to him by prospective customers.

Verdin remained, throughout his life, an avatar of a vanishing era. A descendant of Houma and French ancestors, he spoke the patois French that has all but disappeared from southeast Louisiana. Although his primary income came from carving decoys, he and his family also engaged in trapping—trading pelts for groceries as late as the 1950s—and shrimp trawling.

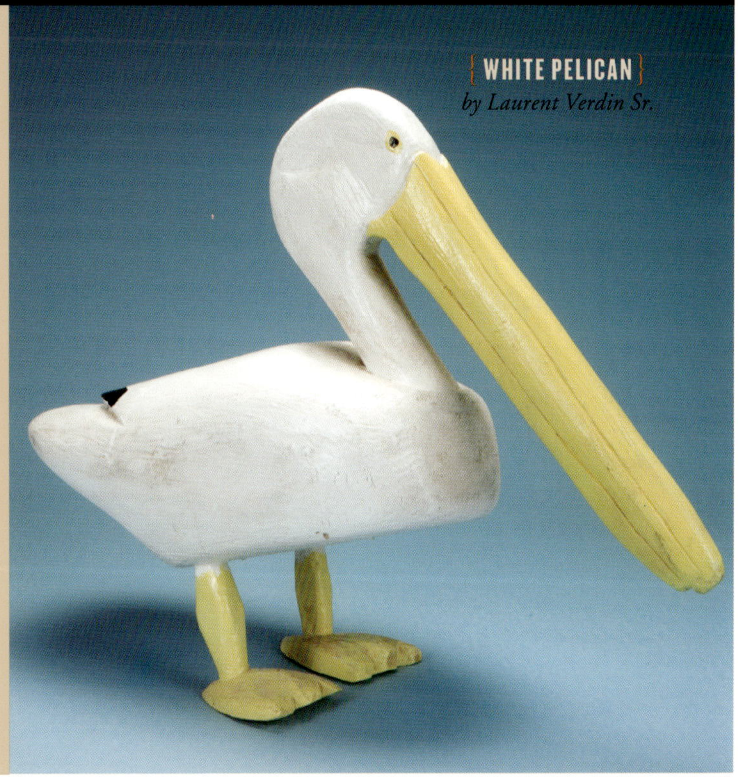

{WHITE PELICAN}
by Laurent Verdin Sr.

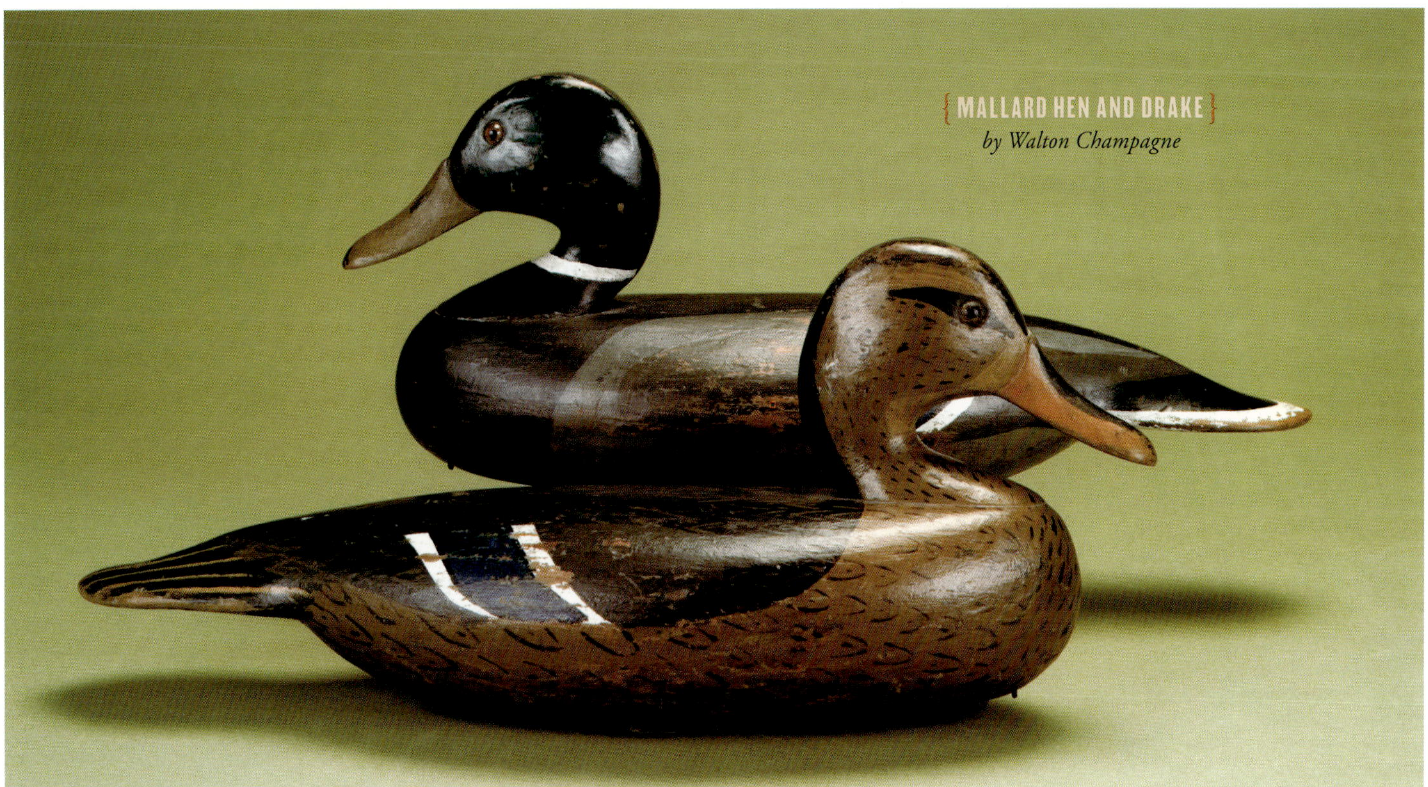

{MALLARD HEN AND DRAKE}
by Walton Champagne

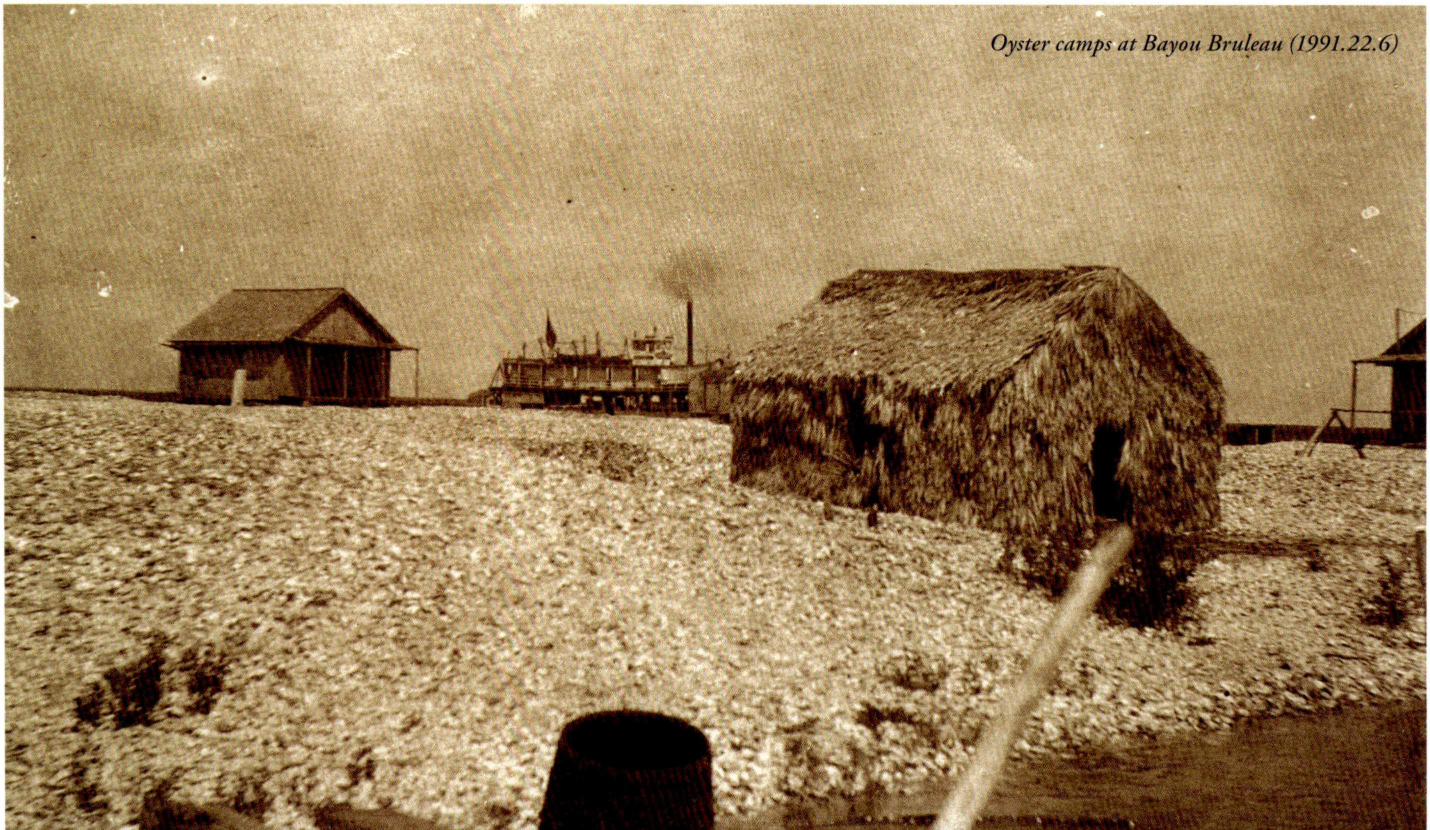

Oyster camps at Bayou Bruleau (1991.22.6)

{ BAYOU LAFOURCHE }

ONCE DESCRIBED AS "Louisiana's longest main street," Bayou Lafourche (from the French for "fork") has long served as a thoroughfare for goods and a corridor for settlement. The bayou wends some 107 miles from the Mississippi River to the Gulf of Mexico, its banks dotted by communities large and small—Donaldsonville, Napoleonville, Raceland, Thibodaux, Larose, Cut Off, Galliano, Golden Meadow. Pirogues and bateaux, once the bayou's principal watercraft, have been replaced over time by shrimp trawlers harvesting crustaceans and by crew boats and drilling rigs servicing the offshore oil and gas industry. Sugar cane, historically an important crop, still grows in abundance, often on tracts of land whose 18th-century boundary lines remain in place.

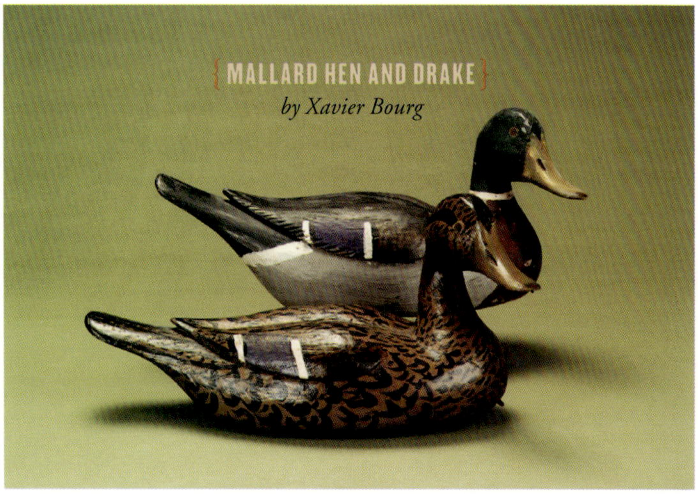

{ MALLARD HEN AND DRAKE }
by Xavier Bourg

As Bayou Lafourche nears the Gulf, the landscape opens up into coastal marsh, a habitat that incubates and sustains the area's bountiful fauna—and shapes the lives of trappers, fishermen, and hunters. A strong carving tradition, developed during the last years of the 19th century, is sustained today by descendants of some of the earliest carving families.

On this eastern edge of Louisiana's Acadian country, French is not spoken nearly as much as it was before World War II, but remnants of the lilting dialect still ring in the names of the area's birds: *poule d'eau, branchier,* and *dos gris* (coot, wood duck, and scaup).

Carvers from the area include **Xavier Bourg, Sidney Foret, Wade LeBlanc, Nedville Martin, Octave Monier, Dewey Pertuit, Theodule "Tatie" Pertuit, Reme Roussel, Joseph Serigny, Beauregard Vizier, Clovis "Cadice" Vizier, Odee "Bee" Vizier,** and **Richard Waguespack.**

{CLOVIS VIZIER}

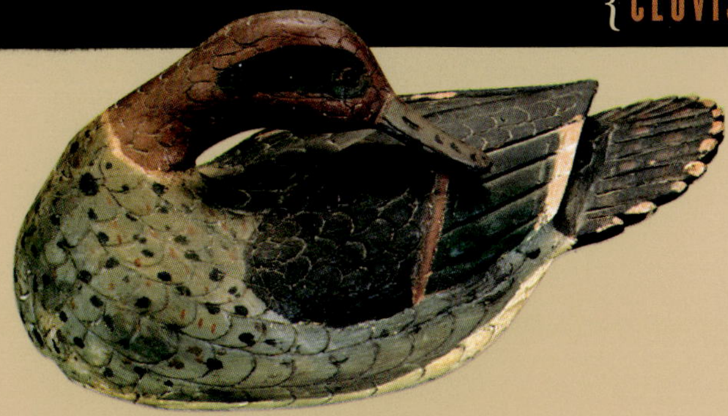

{PREENING GREEN-WINGED TEAL}
by Clovis Vizier

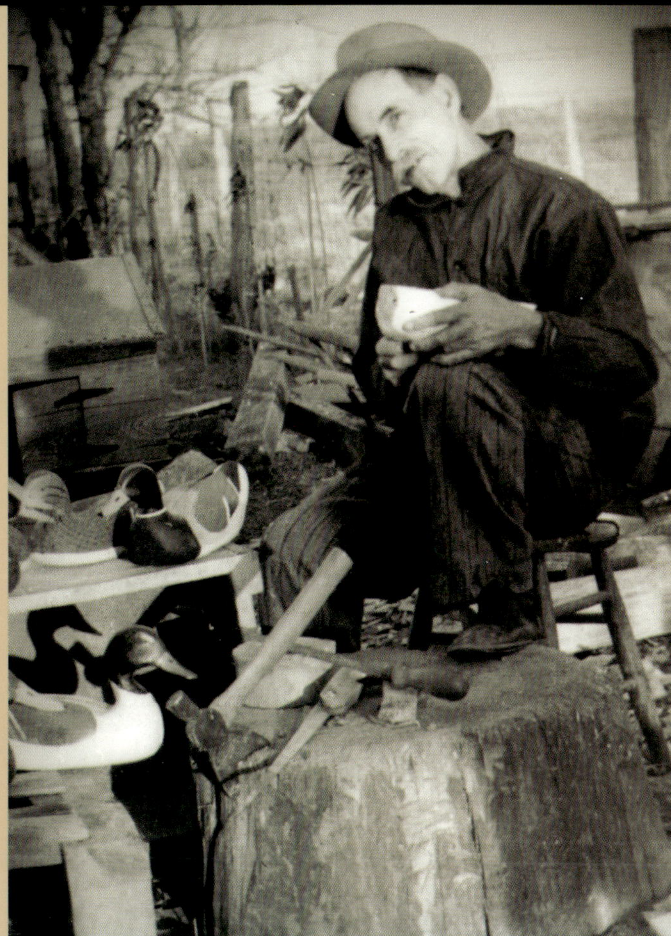

CLOVIS "CADICE" VIZIER (ca. 1885–1975) was born in Chenière Caminada, a small fishing community near Grand Isle. He and the rest of the Vizier clan resettled in Galliano after a hurricane devastated the settlement in October of 1893. Best known for the incised feathering on his decoys and the inclusion of outspread—or fan-shaped—tail feathers, Vizier influenced generations of carvers up and down the Bayou Lafourche. Active for more than half a century, he carved the full range of waterfowl species found in Louisiana. He also produced some of the region's earliest decorative carvings, including eagles; intricately carved and painted miniatures; and mallards, pintails, and wood ducks in flight.

Clovis Vizier, from the collection of Brian Cheramie and David Hall

{PINTAIL DRAKE}
by Clovis Vizier

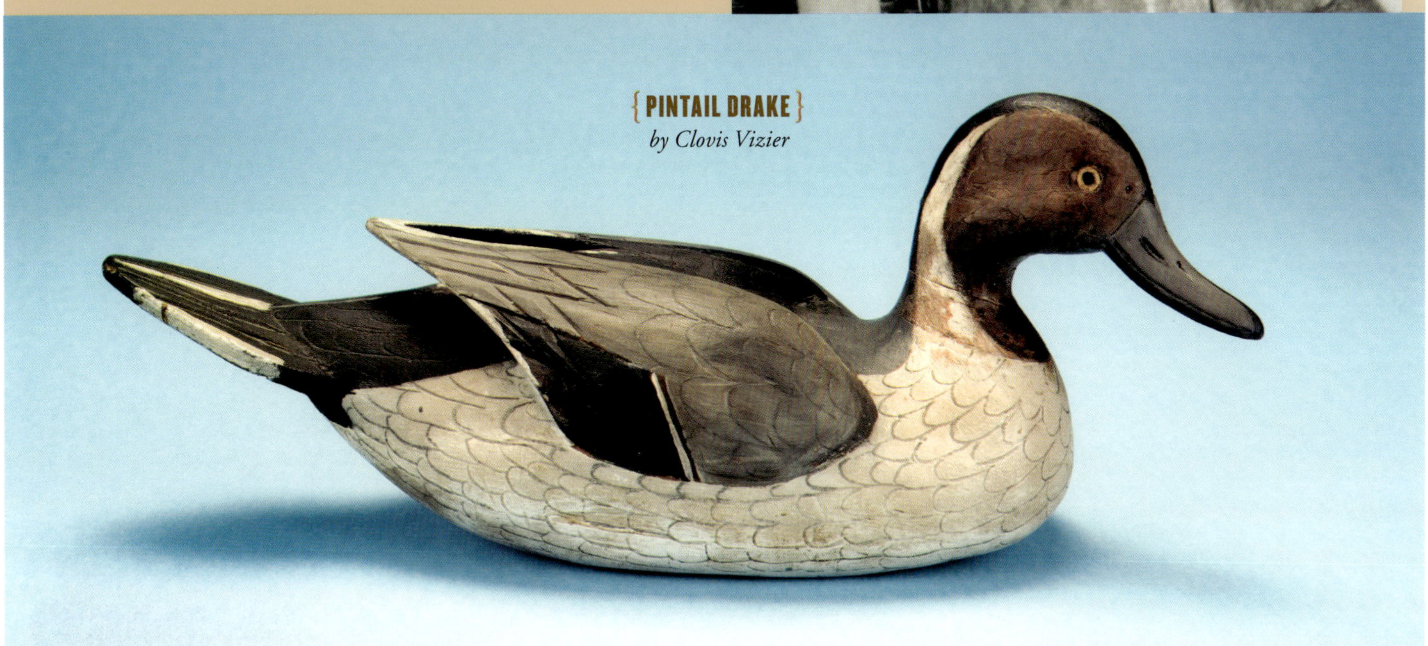

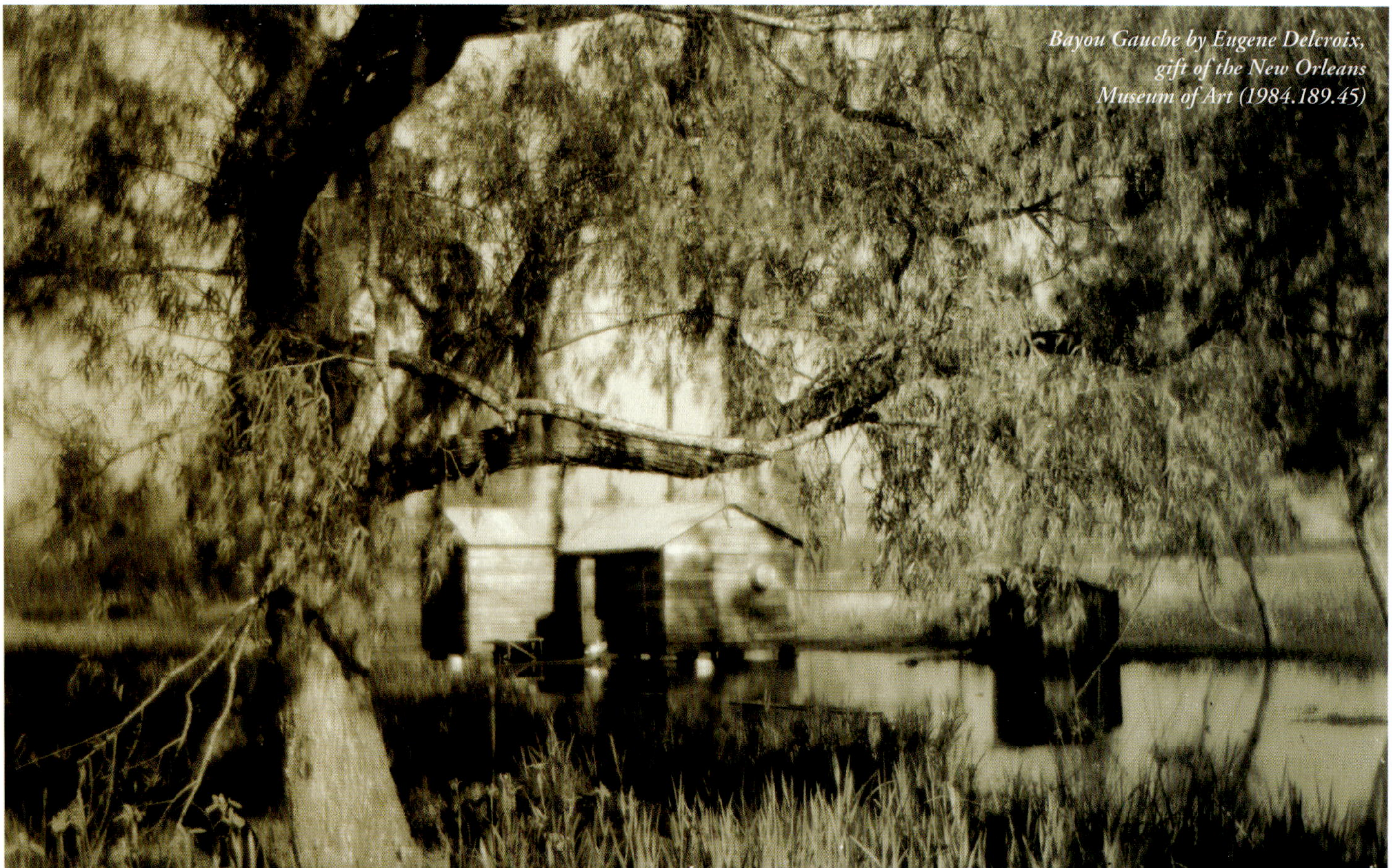

Bayou Gauche by Eugene Delcroix, gift of the New Orleans Museum of Art (1984.189.45)

{LAC DES ALLEMANDS AND BAYOU GAUCHE}

THE GERMAN COAST (Côte des Allemands) stretches along the banks of the Mississippi River above New Orleans. Its name derives from the community formed in the early 1720s by settlers from Europe's Germanic states, recruited to be farmers in the French colony of Louisiana. The enterprise thrived, thanks to the region's rich alluvial soil, and descendants of the original settlers still populate the area around Lac des Allemands and Bayou Gauche.

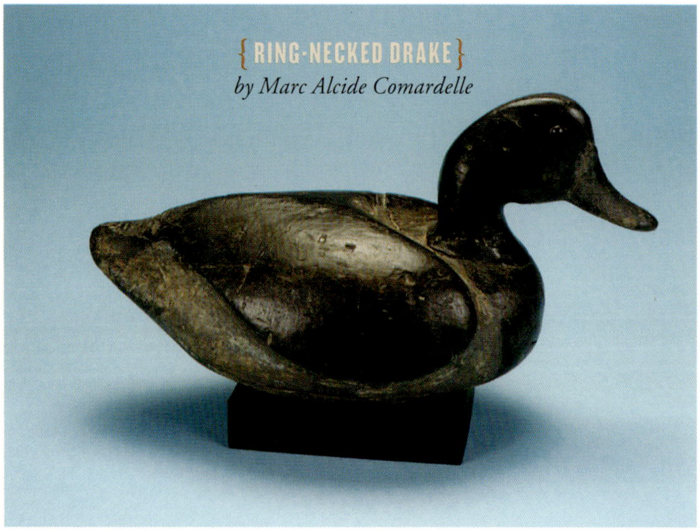

{RING-NECKED DRAKE}
by Marc Alcide Comardelle

A web of bayous, *traînasses,* and larger manmade canals connects the area's many small lakes and ponds. With its proximity to coastal marsh and its position on the Mississippi flyway, the region attracts numerous migratory fowl—and, in turn, avid sport hunters and decoy carvers. At times, hunting on Lake Salvador and other nearby lakes has taken on a less-than-sporting cast. Although the Lacy Act, passed by Congress in 1900, specifically banned the practice of commercial hunting for migratory waterfowl, market hunters working at night could drop dozens of birds with a single shot from their enormous punt guns. In the early years of the 20th century, subsistence hunters and sportsmen were instrumental in having at least one of these guns confiscated by federal game agents.

Carvers of note from the region include **Albert Comardelle, Marc Alcide Comardelle, Frank Dufrene,** and **Eddie Granier.**

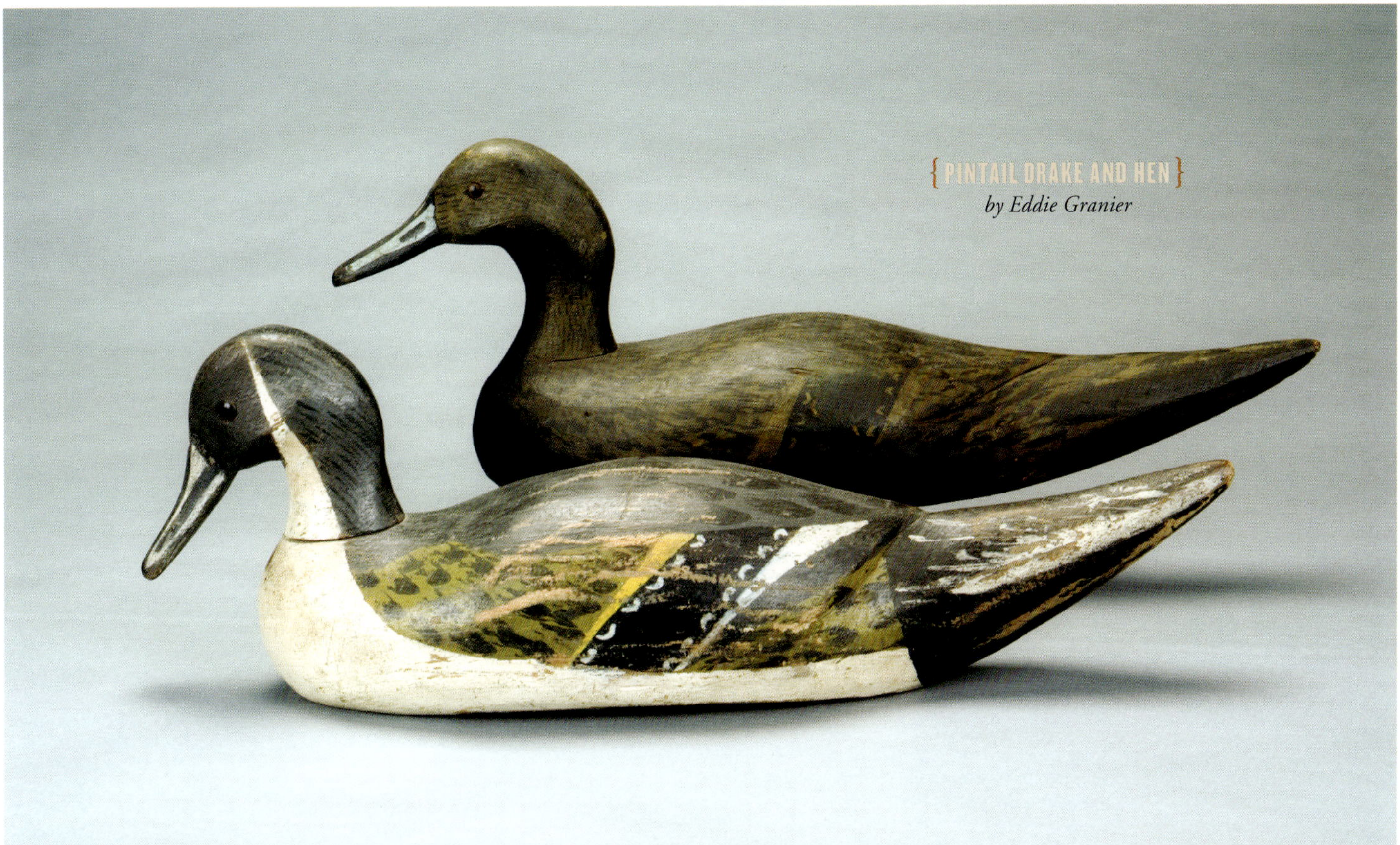

{ PINTAIL DRAKE AND HEN }
by Eddie Granier

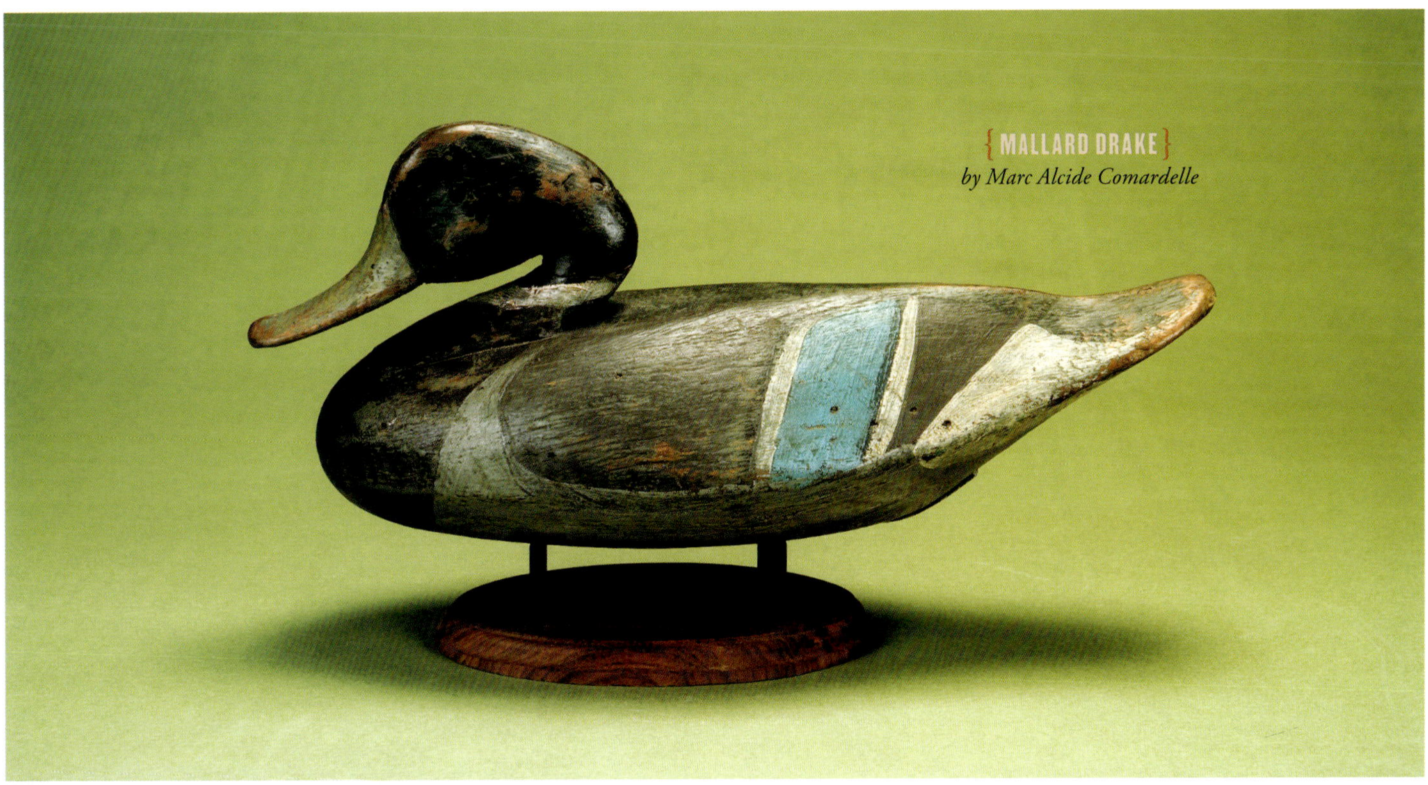

{ MALLARD DRAKE }
by Marc Alcide Comardelle

New Orleans duck hunter, from the collection of Brian Cheramie and David Hall

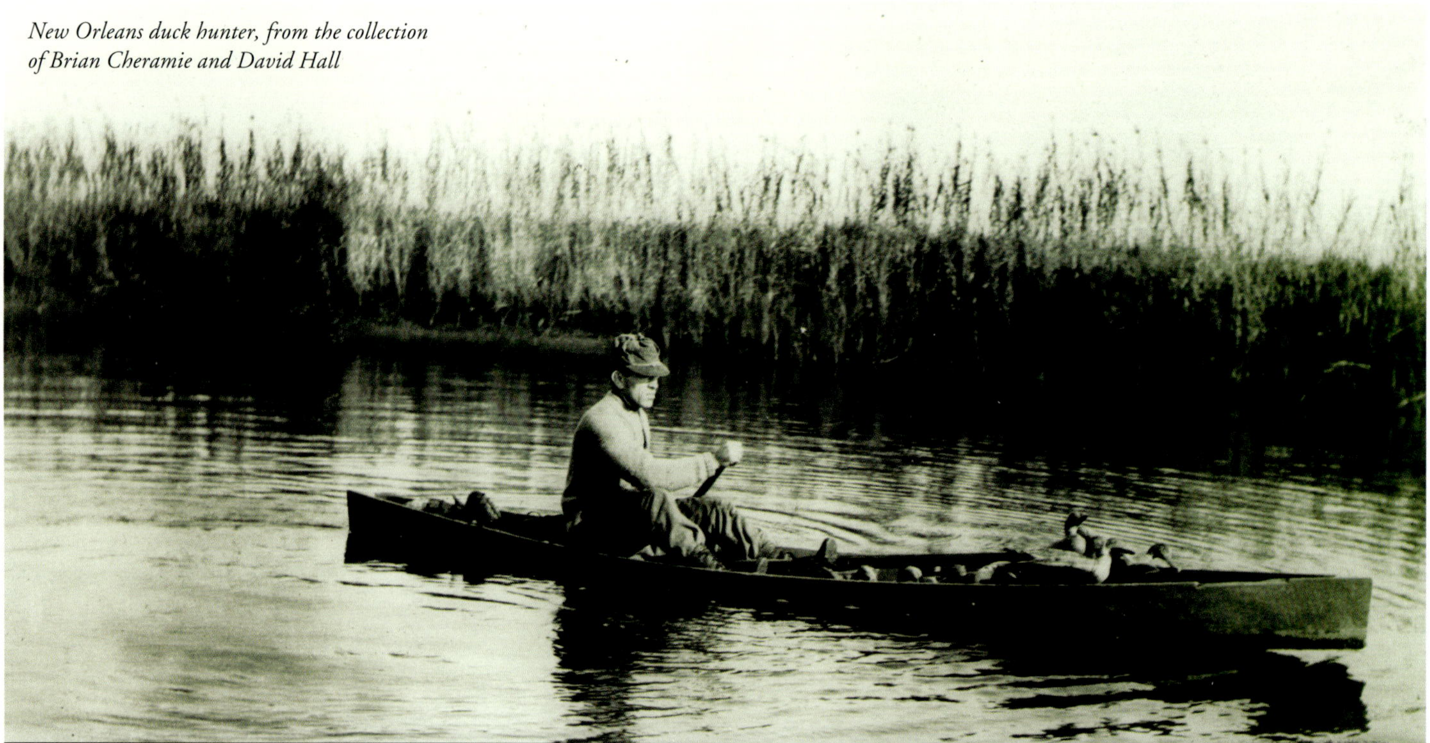

{NEW ORLEANS}

LARGE TRACTS OF MARSHLAND may be found within the city limits of New Orleans, principally on the eastern and northern edges. Although a great deal of marsh acreage was developed for building lots in the second half of the 20th century, substantial portions remain under the protection of the National Parks Service. These lands are embraced by the eastern reaches of Lake Pontchartrain and parts of lakes Catherine and Borgne, and crisscrossed by Chef Menteur Pass, the Rigolets, the Intracoastal Waterway, Irish Bayou, and vestiges of Bayou Sauvage. The development of a local carving tradition was inevitable, given the habitat's appeal to both ducks and sport hunters.

Though New Orleans decoy carvers used the customary blocks of cypress root to carve their birds, these urbanites had a bonus resource in the form of balsa wood. As ships were decommissioned following World War II and broken down for scrap metal in area shipyards, their canvas-covered balsa life rafts were discarded. Carvers eagerly recycled the wooden jetsam into decoys.

Situated on Chef Menteur Pass within the city limits of New Orleans and established in 1815, the Tally-Ho Club is the nation's oldest hunting club. It was one of several private clubs in southeast Louisiana that operated for hunters and sportsmen. Membership included both locals and visitors who came south for the fall and winter hunting seasons.

Regional carvers of note include **Al Beyl, John P. Couret, Robert Couret, Michael Frady, David Hymel, George Morel, Jim Mossmeier, Oscar Murphy, Cassius Peacock, Francis Uzee,** and **John Scott Young.**

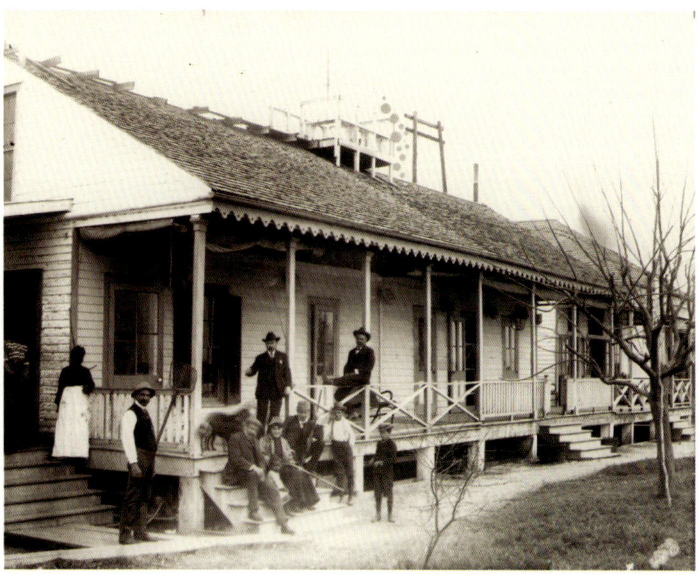

The Tally-Ho Club, from the collection of Brian Cheramie and David Hall

{JOHN P. AND ROBERT COURET}

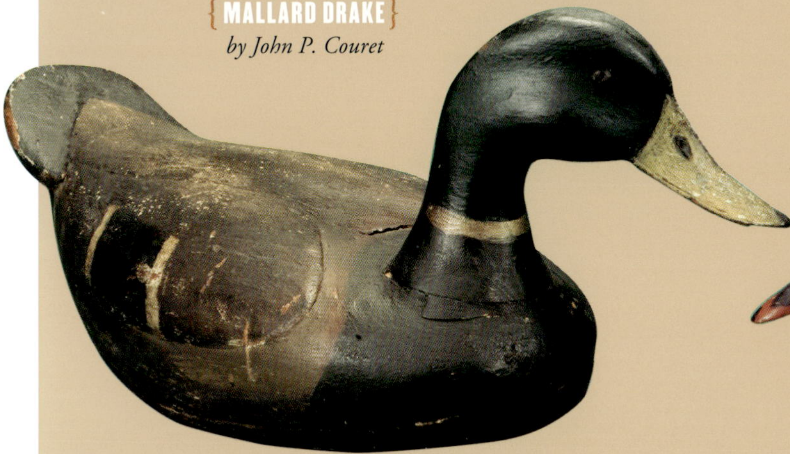

{ MALLARD DRAKE }
by John P. Couret

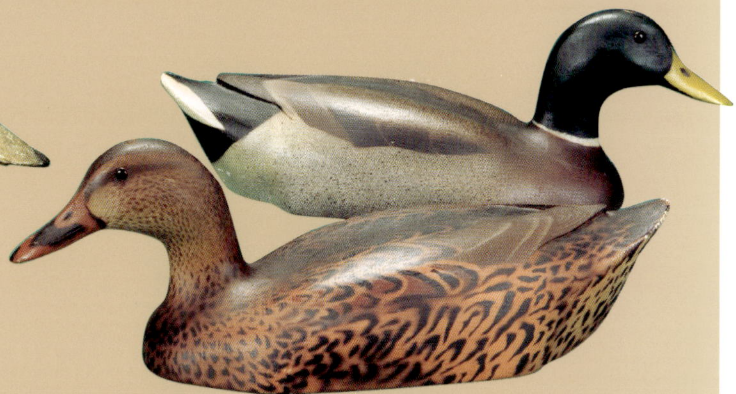

{ MALLARD HEN AND DRAKE }
by Robert Couret, Lifelike Lures

NEW ORLEANS NATIVE John P. Couret (1881–1967) was among the earliest of the Louisiana carvers to elevate the painting of decoys into an art. Inspired by the wildfowl studies of such artists as John James Audubon, Achille Perelli, and George Viavant, Couret produced *nature morte* paintings as well as decoys with detailed paint patterns. His son, Robert Couret (1909–1995), also recognized the aesthetic appeal of detailed decoys. But unlike his father, who carved a small number of decoys exclusively for friends and family, Robert Couret was interested in creating a mechanized process for decoy production. Using his engineering acumen, Couret revolutionized Louisiana decoy carving with the invention of a mass-production technique that, at peak production, could yield an awe-inspiring sixty unpainted ducks in a single day. Though his company, Lifelike Lures, was short-lived, Robert Couret can be seen as an evolutionary link between traditional carvers and decoy factories, whose mass-produced models became increasingly popular after World War II.

{ NORTHERN SHOVELER DRAKE AND HEN }
by Jim Mossmeier

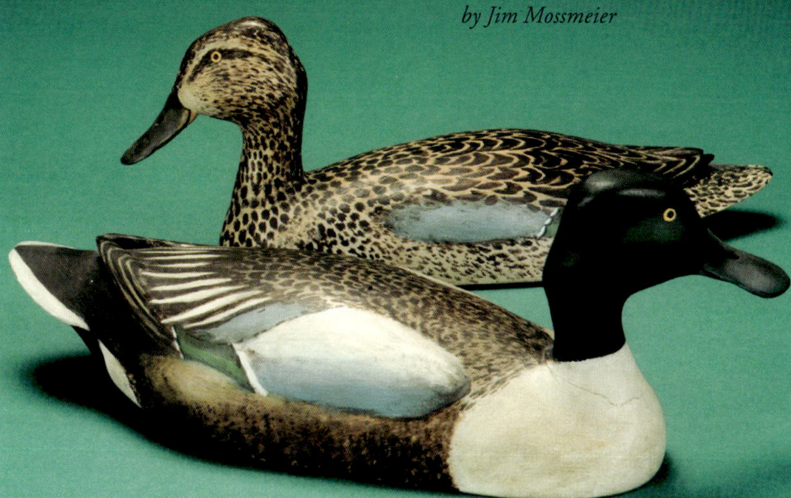

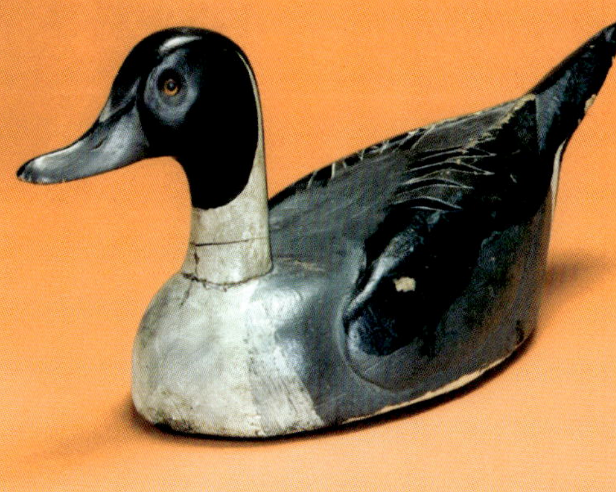

{ PINTAIL DRAKE }
by Al Beyl

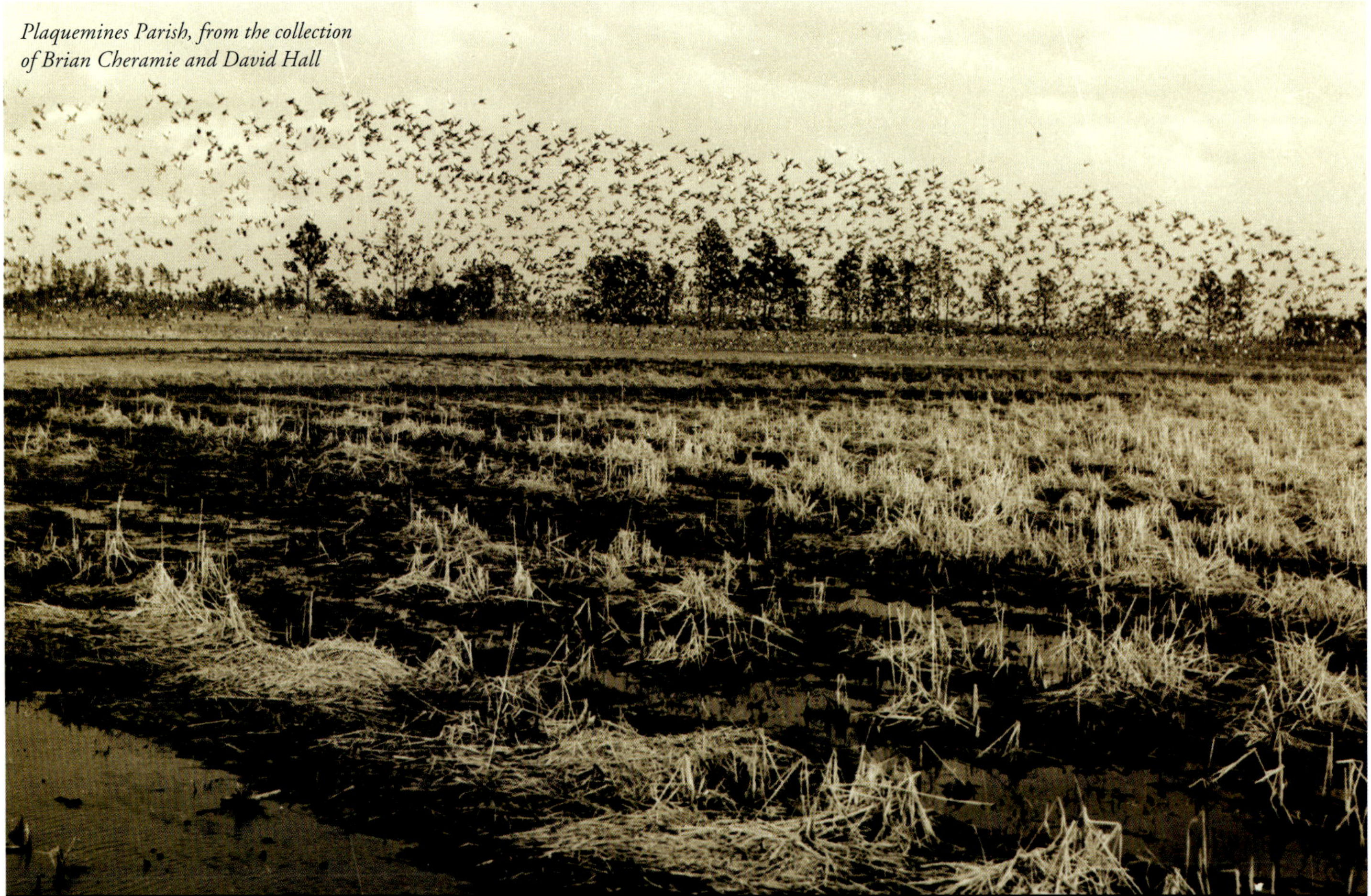

Plaquemines Parish, from the collection of Brian Cheramie and David Hall

{SOUTH OF NEW ORLEANS: UPPER PLAQUEMINES}

LIFE IN UPPER PLAQUEMINES is dominated and divided by the Mississippi River. The powerful waterway snakes its way down the center of the parish, depositing rich soil along its southernmost delta. The northern edge of the parish on the west bank of the river shares a border with New Orleans and stands in stark urban contrast to the increasingly isolated terrain that lies just beyond the town of Belle Chasse. Terraced levees, marshland, and citrus trees bearing Satsuma mandarins, Persian limes, Meyer lemons, and navel oranges line the thin strips of land that flank the river. The towns of Jesuit Bend, Myrtle Grove, Diamond, and Port Sulphur on the west bank, and Bertrandville, Phoenix, Davant, and Pointe a la Hache on the east, rely heavily on citrus and shellfish cultivation and river industries linked to Plaquemines Port to sustain their existence.

That existence is a fragile one for the inhabitants of Plaquemines Parish. Surrounded by water, Upper Plaquemines floods regularly. Communities in the parish have repeatedly faced loss—as was the case in 1927, when 10,000 residents were displaced after New Orleans's business interests convinced the government to dynamite the levees below the city. The waters that swept through the crevasse left much of Plaquemines Parish underwater. More recently, Hurricane Katrina wrought devastating wind and water damage on the majority of structures in the parish.

The same factors that make Upper Plaquemines vulnerable to the elements, however, also make it a haven for diverse wildfowl. Home to more than 40,000 acres of freshwater marsh, Plaquemines Parish has provided a fertile environment for sportsmen. In turn, communities like Phoenix and Davant were home to some of southeast Louisiana's most prominent decoy carvers—who, through the years, supplied both locals and out-of-towners with increasingly detailed "working ducks" for the hunt.

Carvers of note from the region include **Victor Alfonso, Adam Ansardi, John Neville Donewar, Sidney Duplessis, George Frederick Jr., Jules Frederick, Gaston Isadore, Charles Numa Joefrau, Mitchel Lafrance,** and **Matthew Leitel.**

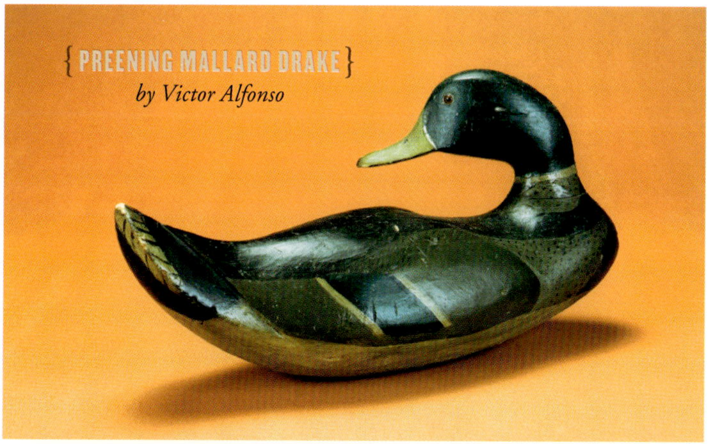

{PREENING MALLARD DRAKE}
by Victor Alfonso

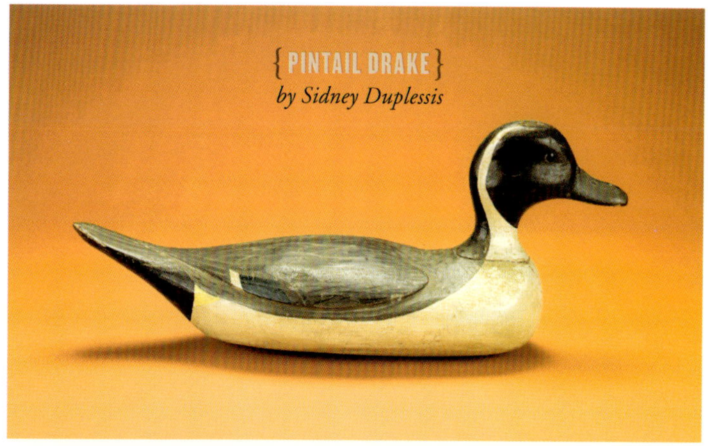

{PINTAIL DRAKE}
by Sidney Duplessis

{MITCHEL LAFRANCE, GEORGE FREDERICK JR., AND CHARLES NUMA JOEFRAU}

PERHAPS THE BEST-KNOWN GROUP of early Louisiana carvers to combine artistic effort with an entrepreneurial spirit was the trio led by Plaquemines Parish native Mitchel Lafrance (1882–1979). Located just upriver from Pointe a la Hache, the hamlets of Phoenix and Davant boast a rich carving heritage. The technique of scratch painting, later a signature Lafrance touch, originated locally, finding expression in the work of pioneers such as Gaston Isadore (1871–1932) and Jules Frederick (1870–1954). Lafrance absorbed, and transcended, local traditions. By the 1920s he had developed a sophisticated carving style that would serve as a model for his generation. A savvy businessman, he would make the most of his collaborations—both formal and informal—with other artists. During the Great Depression, Lafrance found a market for his decoys in retail outlets such as the New Orleans-based Deluca and Lanasa hardware stores. By the late 1930s, he had entered into partnership with his nephew George Frederick Jr. (1907–1977) and his New Orleans neighbor Charles Numa Joefrau (1913–1983). The trio's intricately painted decoys, the majority marketed under the "Lafrance" name, fetched high wholesale prices in New Orleans. Late in life, Lafrance delegated some of the painting of decoys to family members, including his niece Marguerite Hilaire, his nephew August Frederick, and his neighbors Charles, Rudy, and Eric Hutchison.

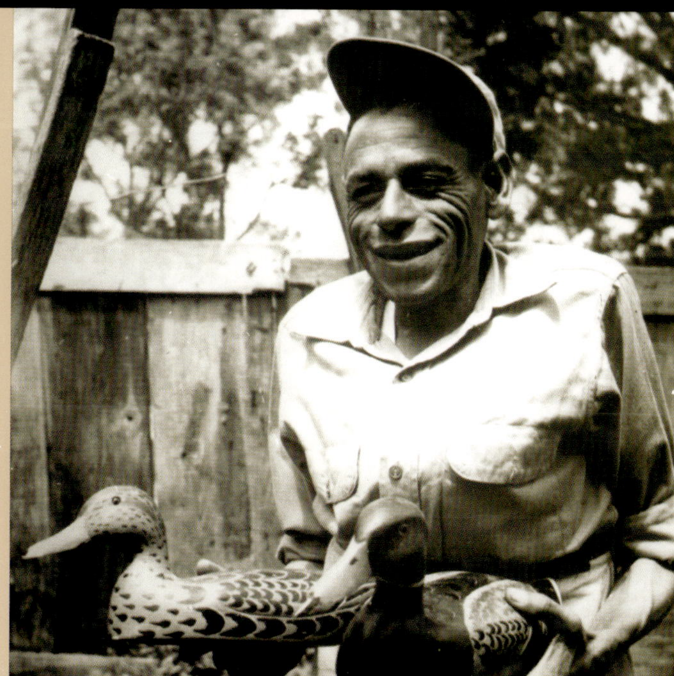

Charles Numa Joefrau, from the collection of Brian Cheramie and David Hall

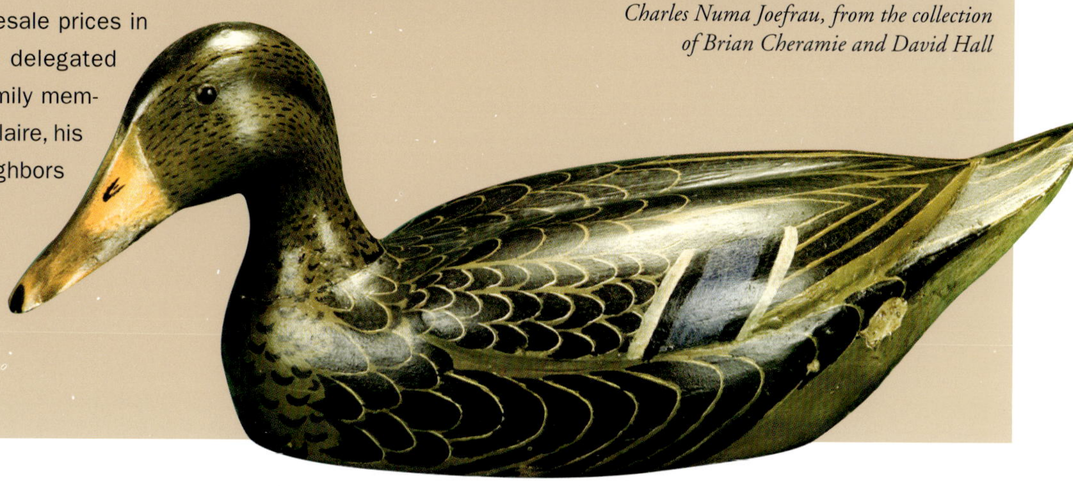

{AMERICAN BLACK DUCK}
(black mallard) by Mitchel Lafrance, Charles Numa Joefrau, and George Frederick Jr.

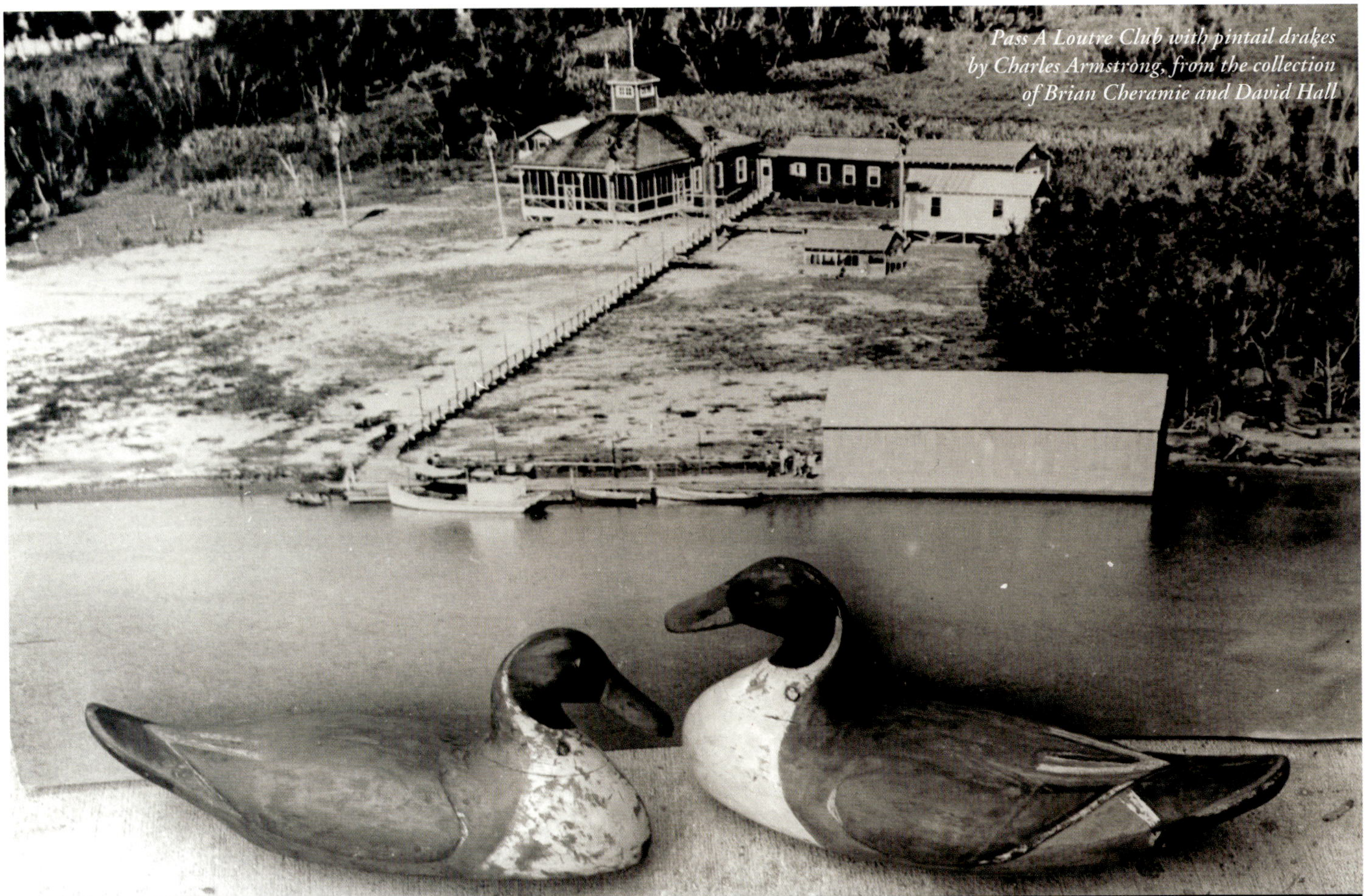

Pass A Loutre Club with pintail drakes by Charles Armstrong, from the collection of Brian Cheramie and David Hall

{MOUTH OF THE MISSISSIPPI: LOWER PLAQUEMINES}

LOWER PLAQUEMINES PARISH follows the course of the Mississippi River from the town of Nairn to the Gulf of Mexico, just beyond Pilottown. At its mouth, the Mississippi unleashes a torrent of water—more than 400,000 cubic feet per second—into the Gulf.

The brackish waterways and marshlands of Lower Plaquemines are considered one of the best destinations for sportsmen eager to take advantage of the region's diverse and bountiful population of migratory waterfowl.

In the first half of the 20th century, hunting clubs like the Delta Duck Club, Joseph Leiter's Chateau Canard Hunting Club, and the Pass A Loutre Club attracted sportsmen from across the country in pursuit of some of the nation's best duck hunting. Local individuals such as **Charles "Napoleon" Armstrong,** a lighthouse keeper at Southwest Pass, often supplemented their income by serving as guides to sportsmen. Guides like Armstrong and **Nicole Vidacovich** sold rigs of decoys to out-of-towners for the hunt and miniature decorative decoys as souvenirs.

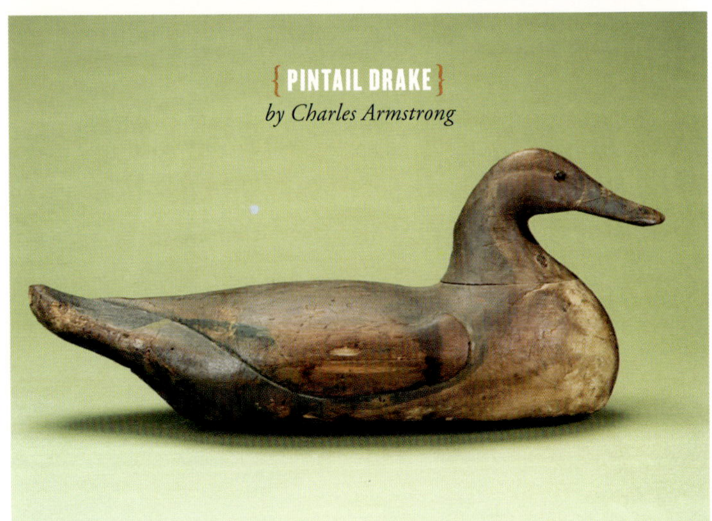

{PINTAIL DRAKE}
by Charles Armstrong

Additional carvers of note from the region include **Hyacinthe Scobel** and **Arthur John Dugar**.

{NICOLE VIDACOVICH}

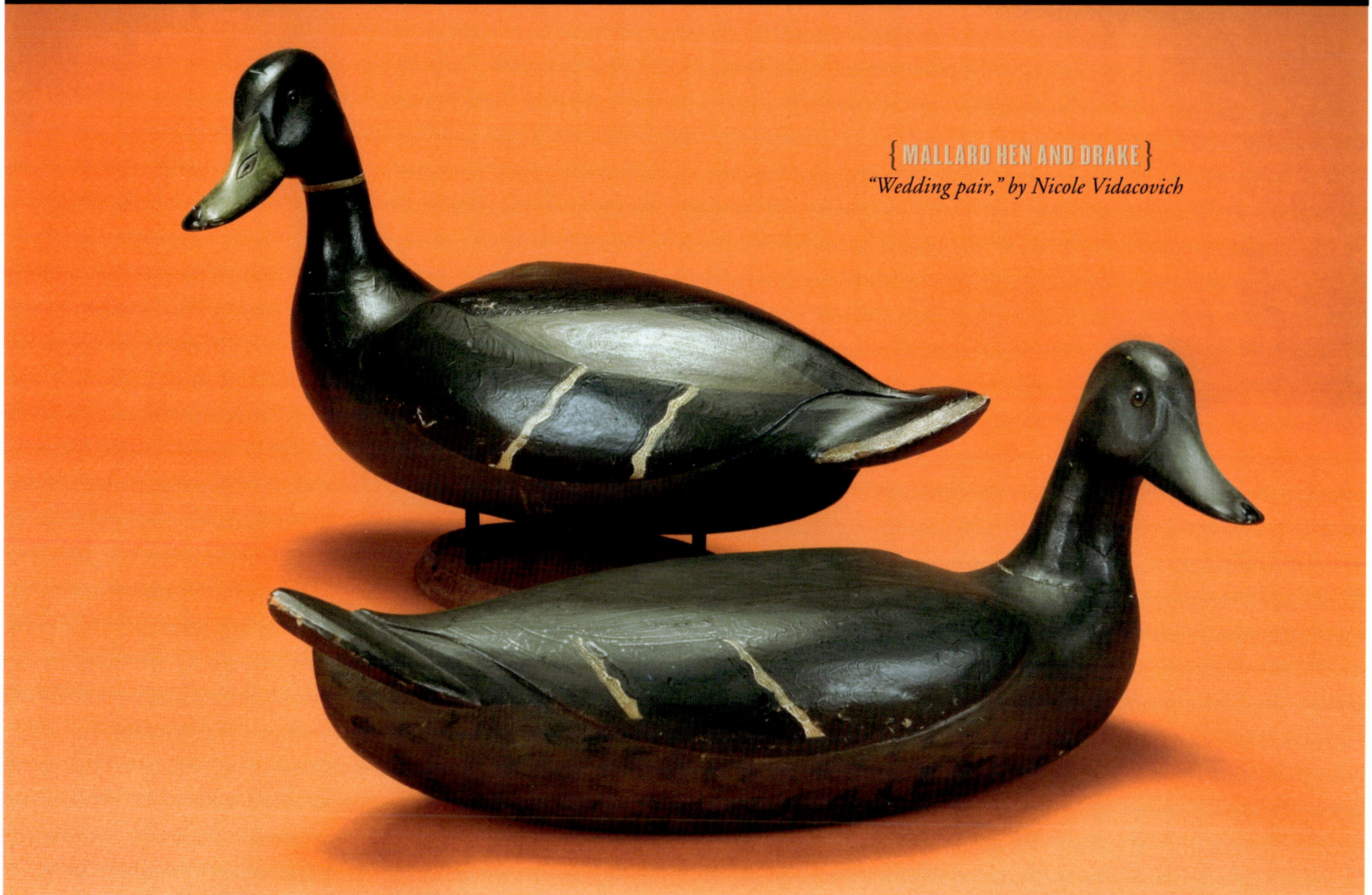

{MALLARD HEN AND DRAKE}
"Wedding pair," by Nicole Vidacovich

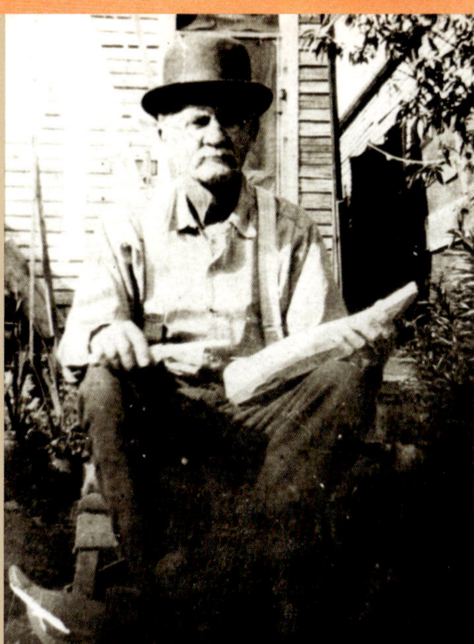

NICOLE VIDACOVICH (1853–1945) of Sunrise, Louisiana, carved some of the most memorable early working decoys. The son of a Yugoslavian carpenter, Vidacovich paid close attention to detail. His use of patterns, artist-grade oil paint, and imported taxidermy-grade glass eyes suggests that Vidacovich may have sensed the potential for decoys to transcend their functional status and, one day, be recognized as a legitimate art form. Vidacovich's desire to extend the parameters of the craft is evidenced by his creation of what can only be described as decorative waterfowl decoys. In the late 1800s, Vidacovich honored his bride-to-be, Mani Bulot, with an oversized pair of stylized, intricately painted mallards. The "wedding pair," as they came to be called, sat on the Vidacovich mantel throughout the couple's marriage.

Nicole Vidacovich, from the collection of Brian Cheramie and David Hall

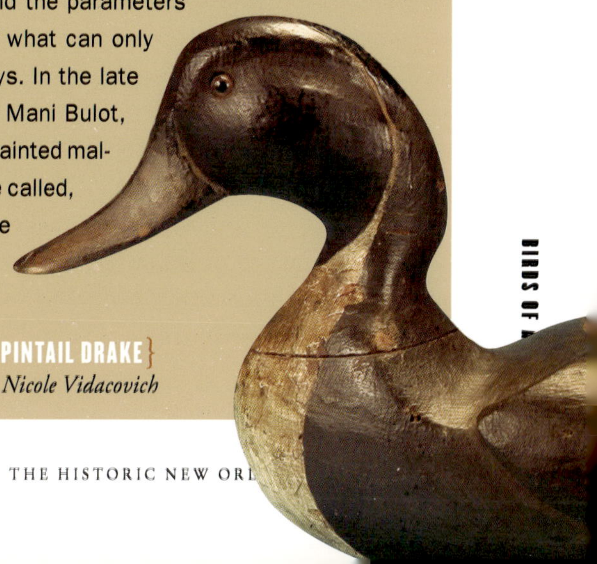

{PINTAIL DRAKE}
by Nicole Vidacovich

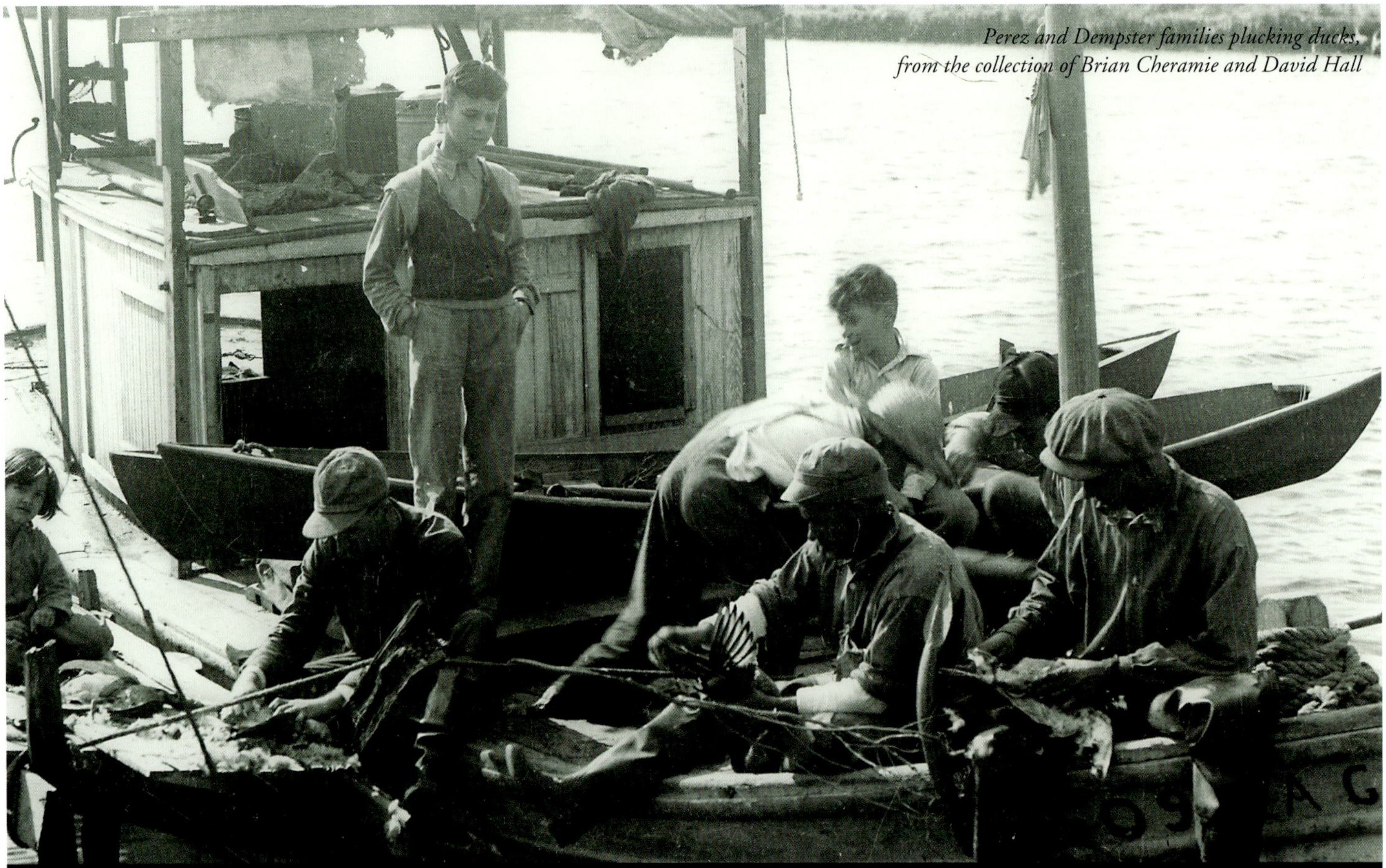

Perez and Dempster families plucking ducks, from the collection of Brian Cheramie and David Hall

{EAST OF NEW ORLEANS TO SHELL BEACH}

ST. BERNARD PARISH, an area that stretches from Jackson Barracks to the shores of Lake Borgne and Breton Sound, is a study in contrasts. The westernmost part of the parish lies minutes from the French Quarter, and New Orleans has long drawn part of its workforce from towns like Chalmette and Arabi. But just beyond the densely populated areas that border Orleans Parish, St. Bernard unfolds into a series of smaller communities whose contours are dominated by marsh and waterways. Home to a sizable enclave of Isleños—individuals of Spanish descent who immigrated to Louisiana from the Canary Islands in the last quarter of the 18th century—the western half of St. Bernard Parish houses the communities of Shell Beach, Delacroix, Hopedale, and Yscloskey.

A bountiful habitat for oystermen, shrimpers, and duck hunters, the marshlands and waterways of St. Bernard Parish have proved particularly vulnerable to tropical storms and hurricanes. In the past hundred years, more than a dozen powerful storms have swept across the parish, claiming lives and homes and washing away much of the work done by local carvers.

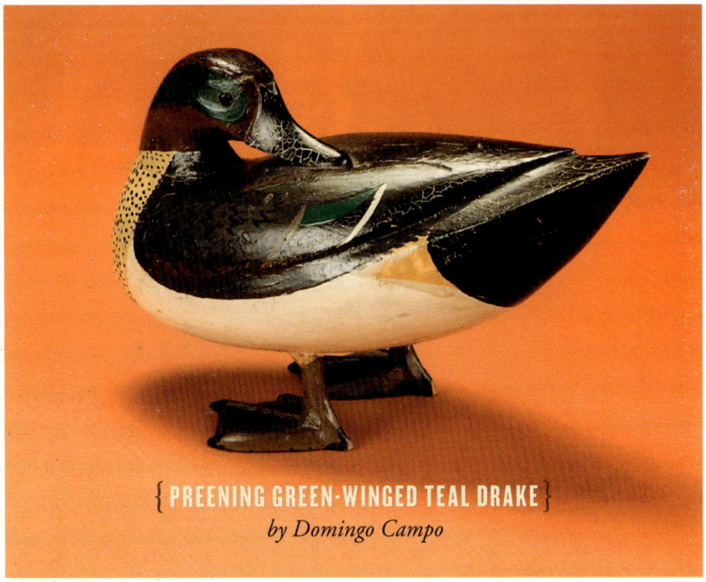

{PREENING GREEN-WINGED TEAL DRAKE}
by Domingo Campo

Carvers of note from the region include **Domingo Campo, Denis Pereira, Omar Perez, James Curtis Roussel,** and **Antonaise St. Germain.**

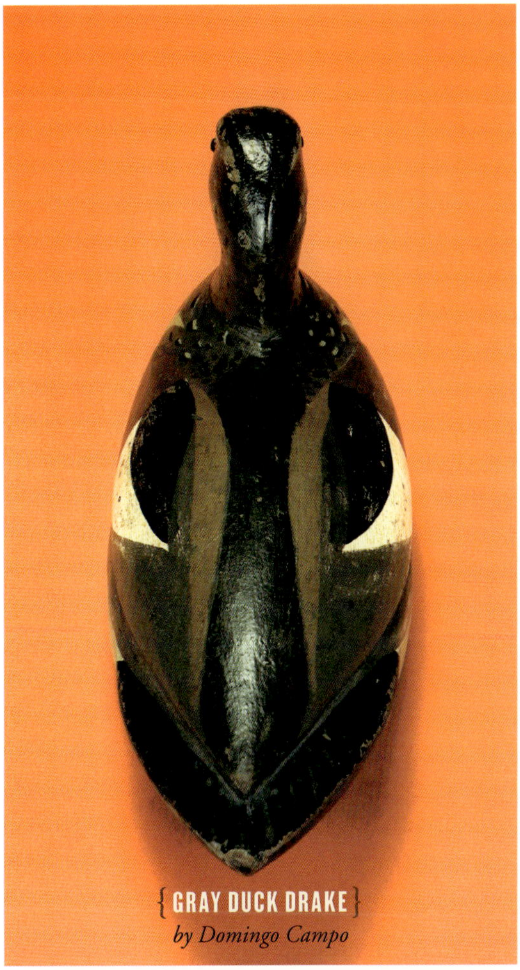

{GRAY DUCK DRAKE}
by Domingo Campo

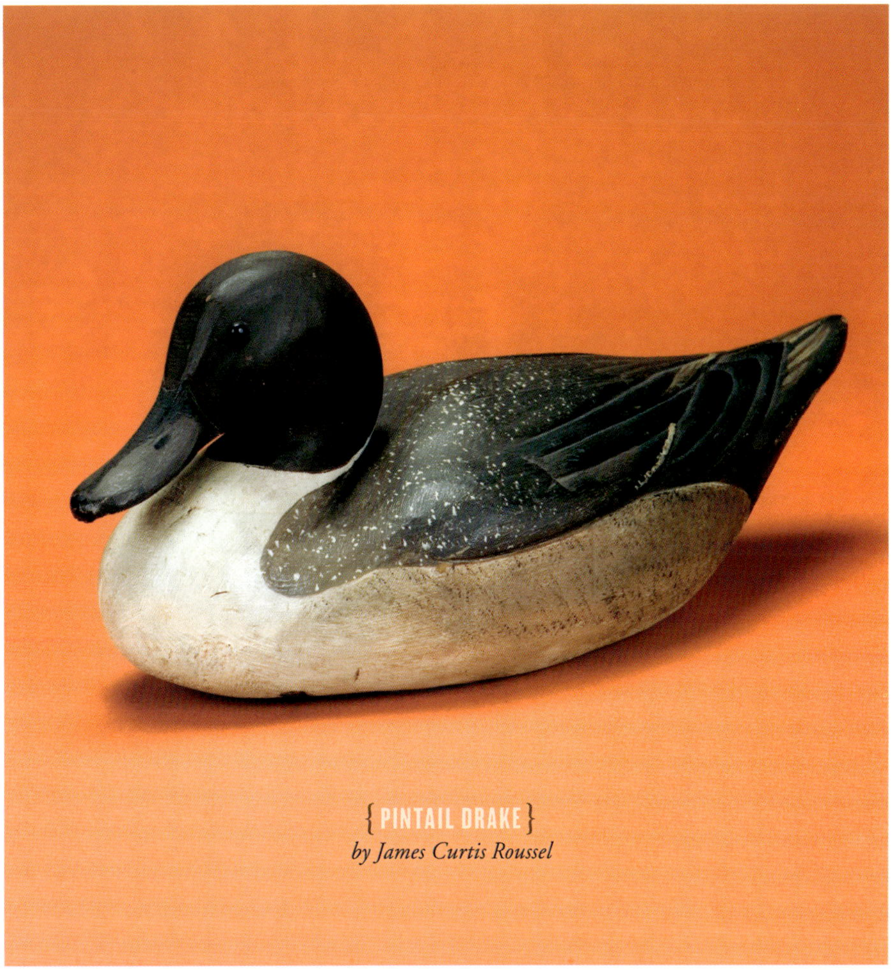

{PINTAIL DRAKE}
by James Curtis Roussel

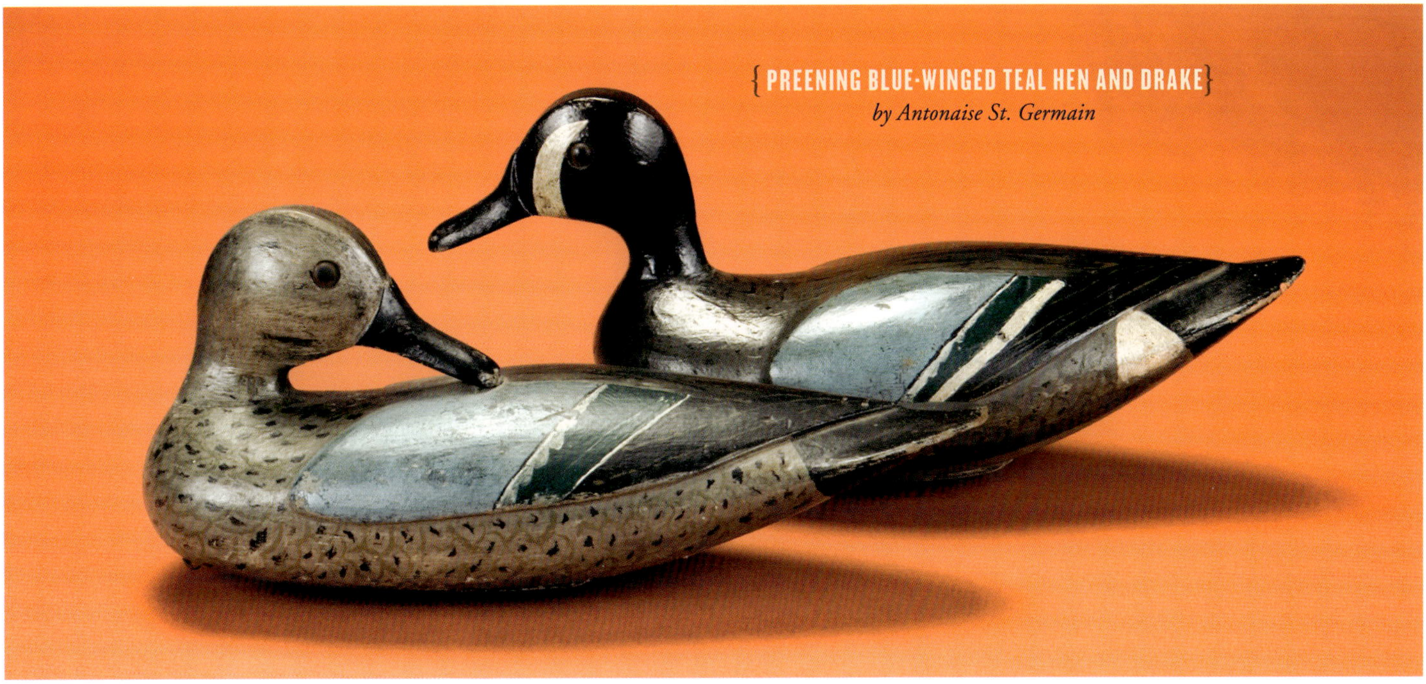

{PREENING BLUE-WINGED TEAL HEN AND DRAKE}
by Antonaise St. Germain

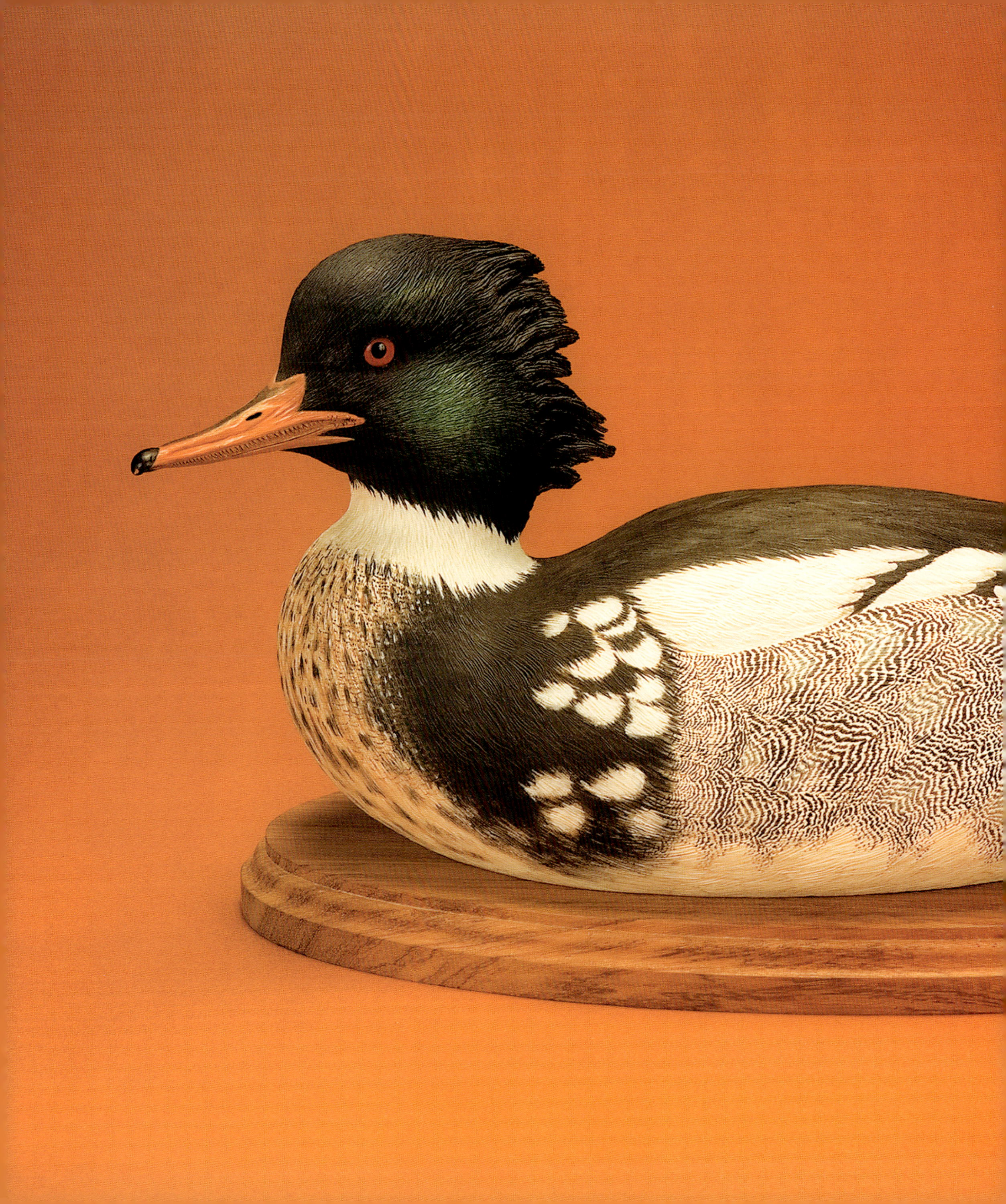

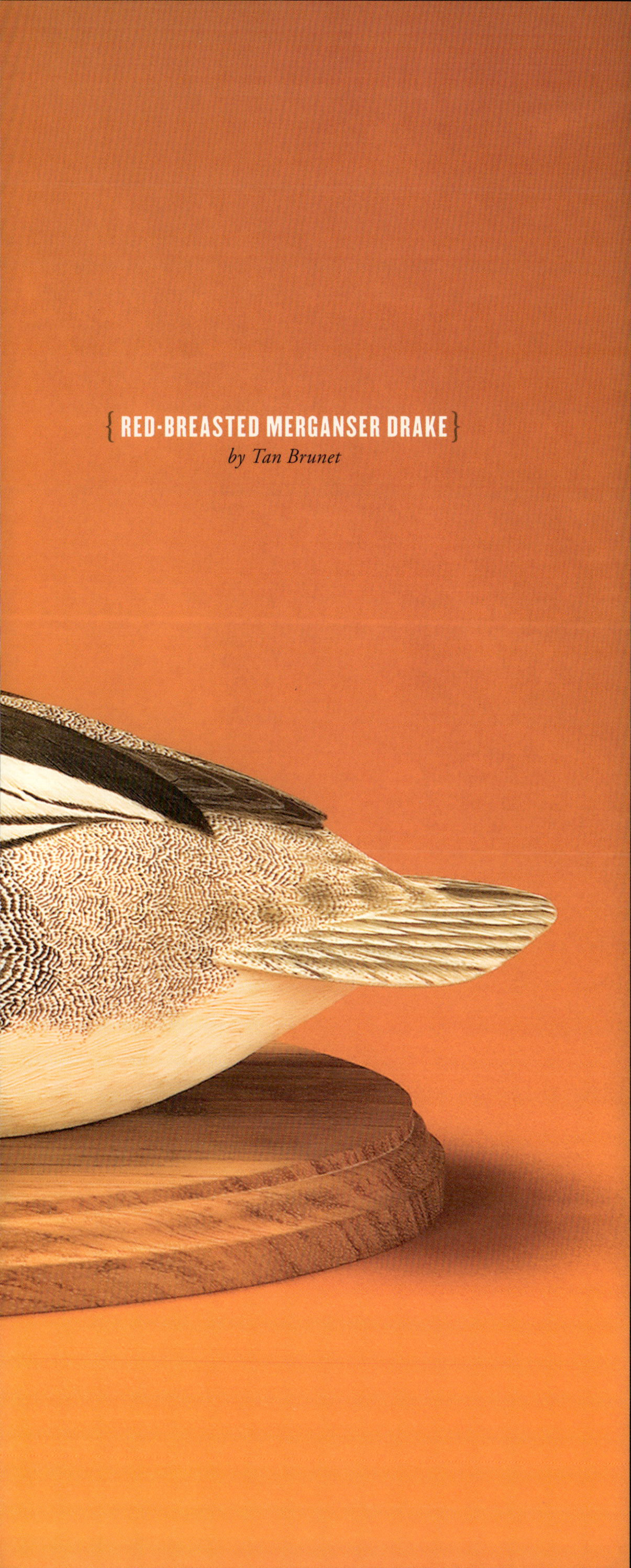

{RED-BREASTED MERGANSER DRAKE}
by Tan Brunet

{BIRDS OF A FEATHER}

Wildfowl Carving in Southeast Louisiana

PART 2

CONTEMPORARY CARVINGS

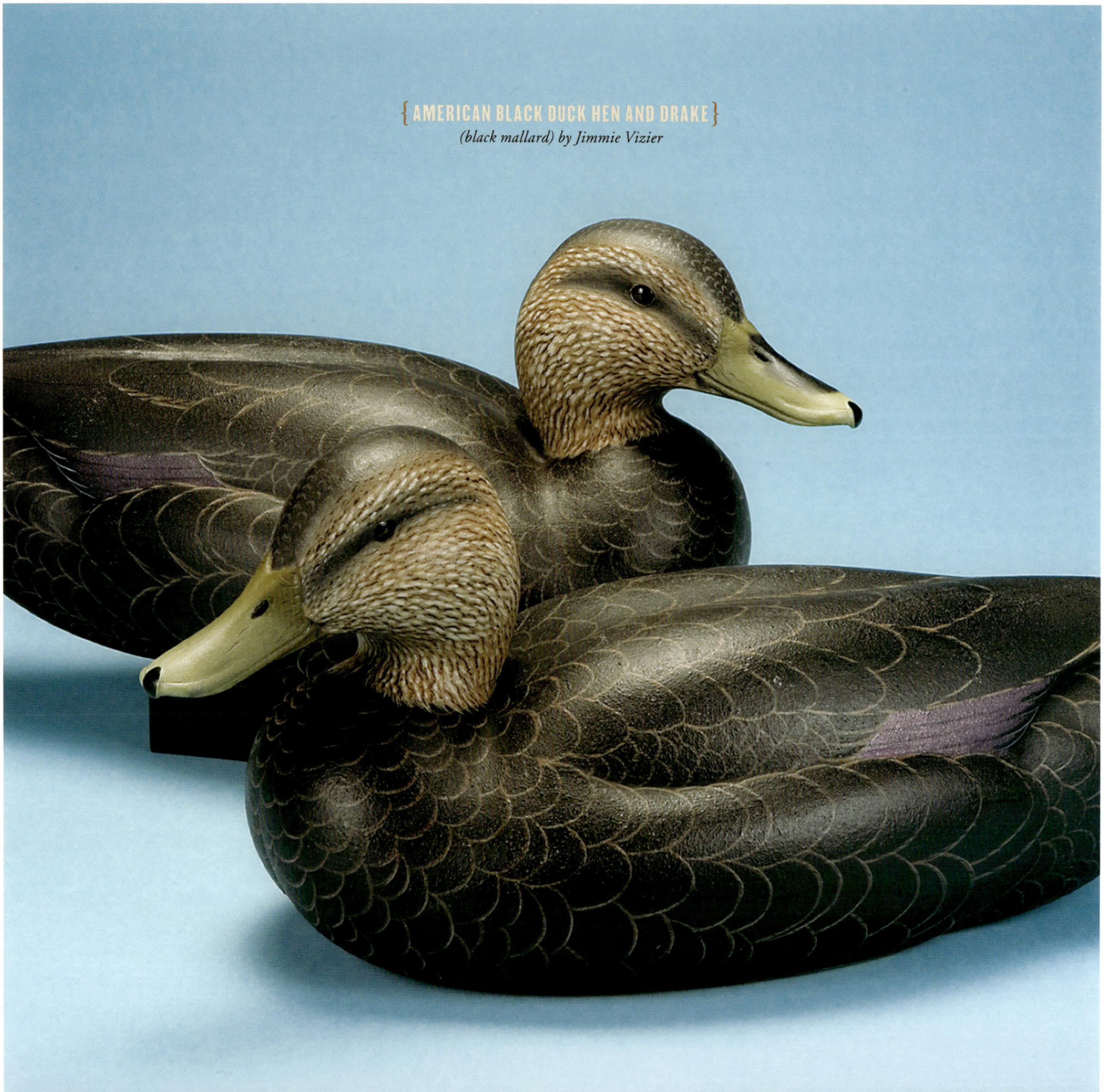

{AMERICAN BLACK DUCK HEN AND DRAKE}
(black mallard) by Jimmie Vizier

{GALLIANO'S DECORATIVE CARVERS}

NEAR WHERE State Highway 308 ends, on the east bank of Bayou Lafourche, lies the town of Galliano. A hummock of land supports the road and its fringe of building lots, then quickly drops off into the marshes. Though small in size, Galliano looms large in the annals of Louisiana decoy carving. **JIMMIE VIZIER** resides here, a decorative carver whose father, uncle, and grandfather achieved renown as makers of working decoys.

Galliano is also home to the Brunet family. The two generations—

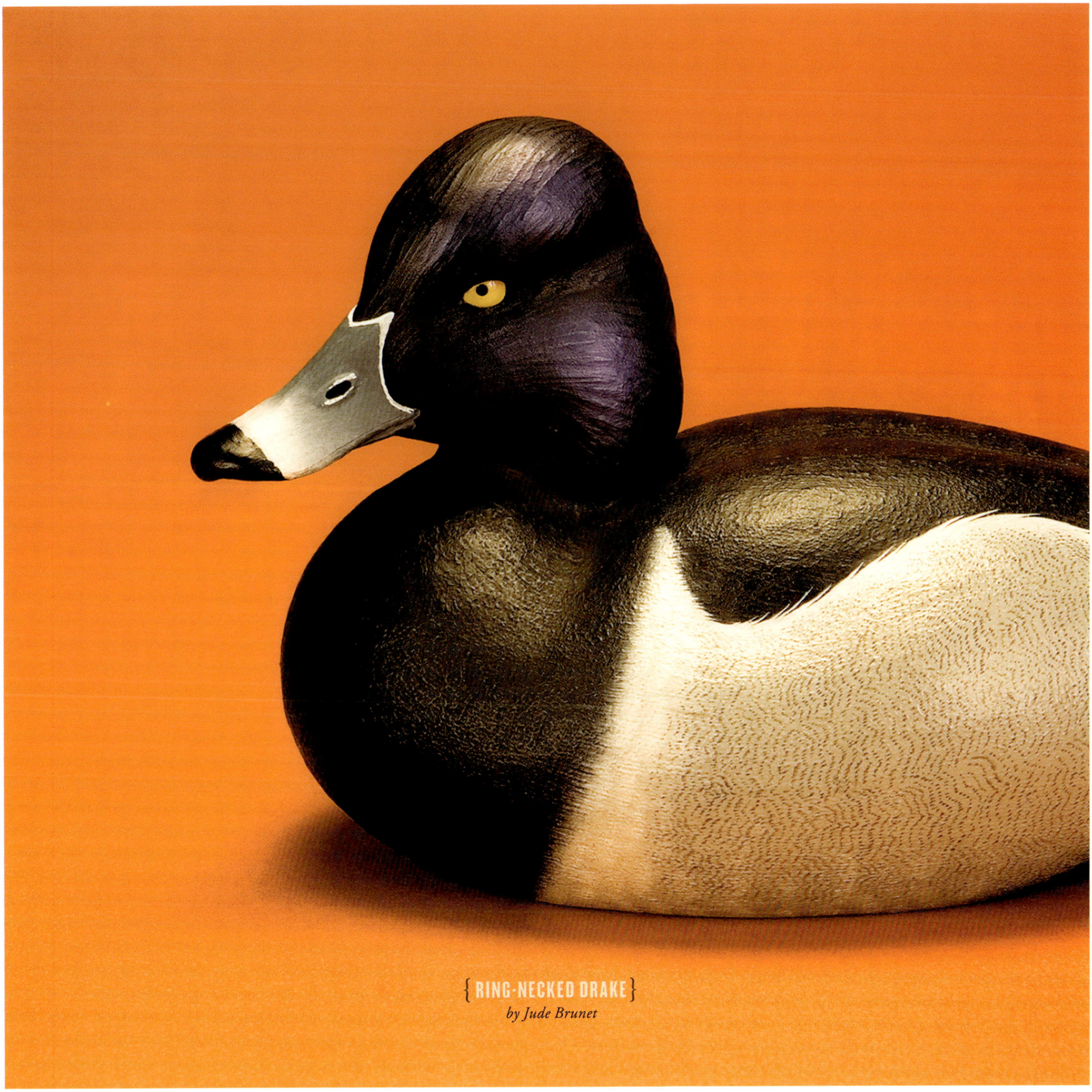

{ RING-NECKED DRAKE }
by Jude Brunet

TAN BRUNET and his sons **JETT** and **JUDE**—have pursued decoy carving and wildlife art with unmatched passion and dedication. Whether Tan Brunet is carving a duck or crafting a paddle or dugout pirogue, there is always a story attached—literally. The senior Brunet takes delight in inscribing personal dedications, historical notes, and other comments on his creations before signing the pieces. Jett Brunet's skills as a decorative carver have been recognized by repeated success in international competitions. Jude, who began his career as a carver, now concentrates on paintings of wildfowl. His lesser scaup pair was the basis for Louisiana's duck stamp in 2000.

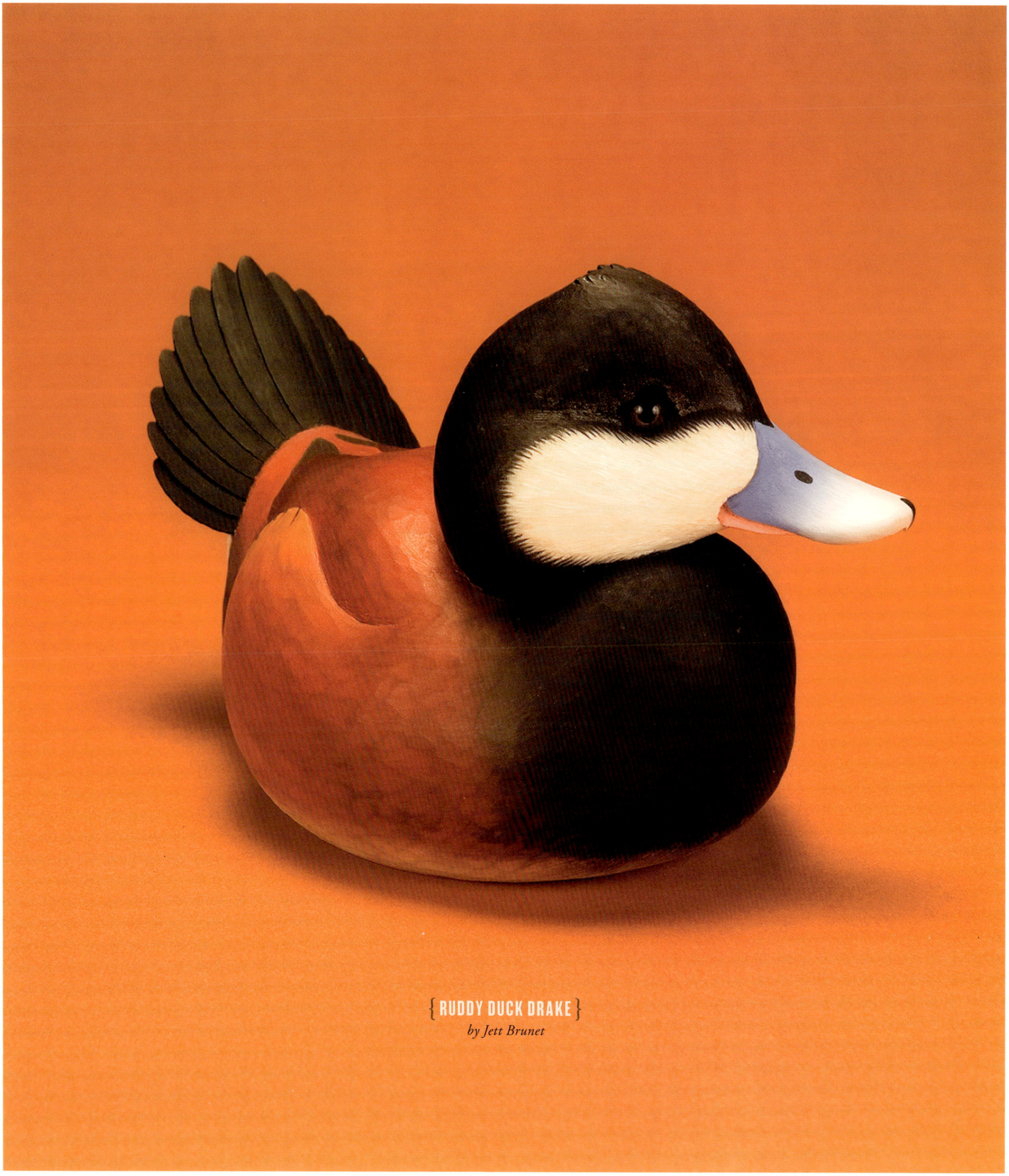

{ RUDDY DUCK DRAKE }
by Jett Brunet

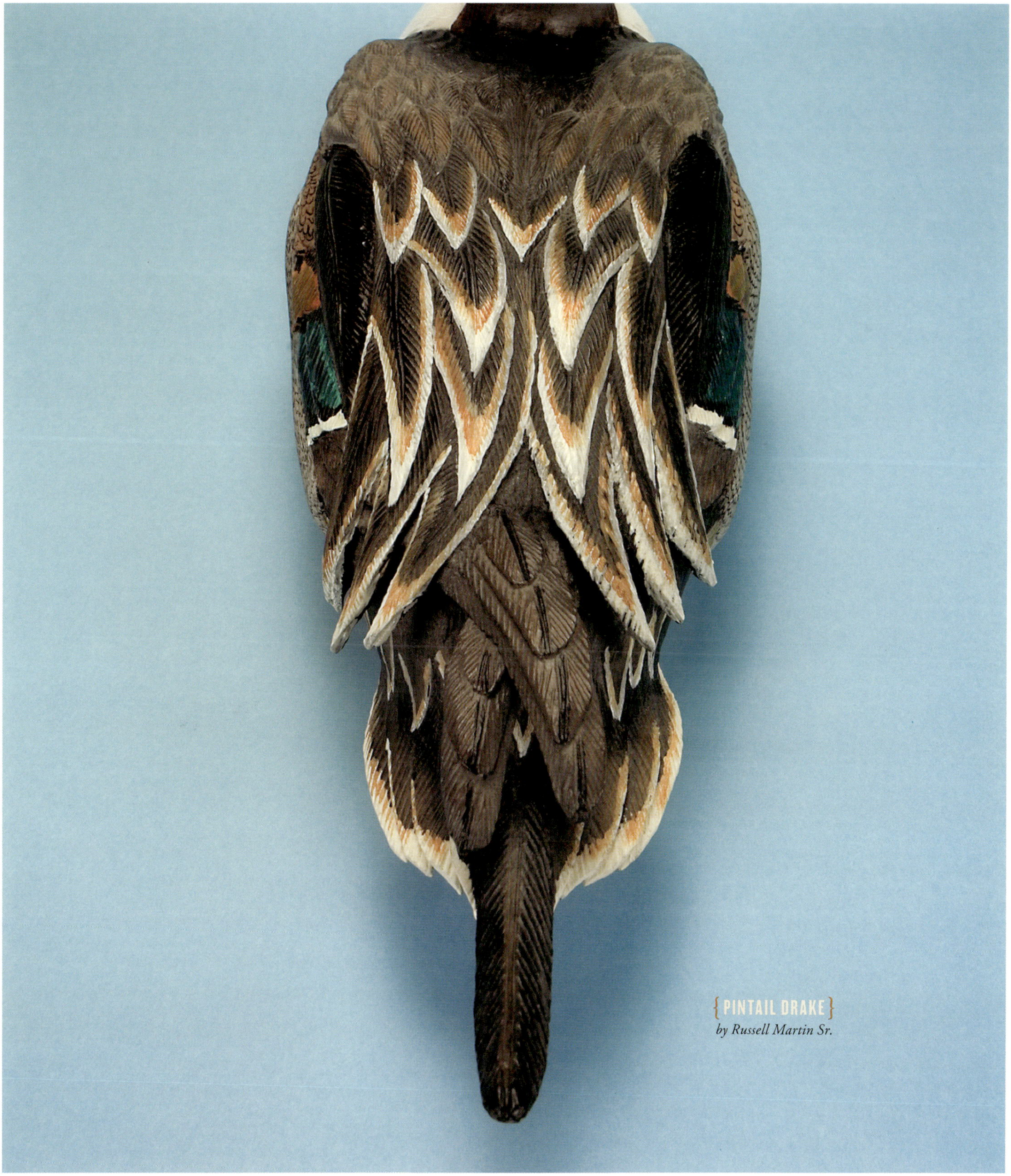

{ PINTAIL DRAKE }
by Russell Martin Sr.

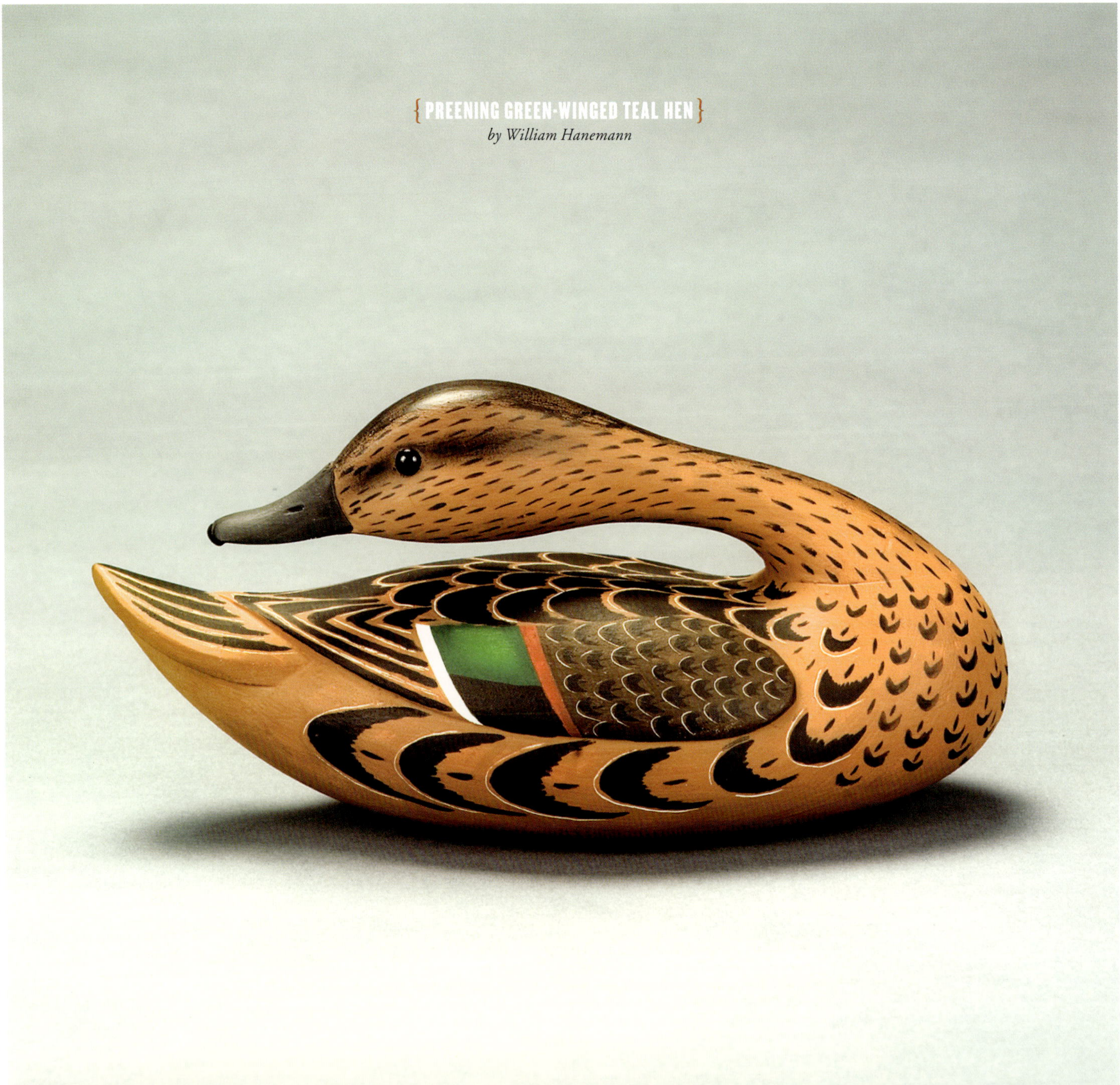

{A CARVER INSPIRED BY A COLLECTOR: WILLIAM HANEMANN}

WILLIAM HANEMANN'S work marks the confluence of two decoy-carving traditions in southeast Louisiana. Early on, Hanemann's career was launched through a synergy of formal and informal educational experiences—industrial arts classes in the New Orleans public schools, coupled with weekly visits to the office of his uncle, the prominent New Orleans decoy collector Jimmie Hanemann. Regular exposure to his uncle's extensive collection inspired William's initial efforts to incorporate the carving and painting techniques of an earlier generation into his own creations.

At age 17, Hanemann was selling miniature decoys through local

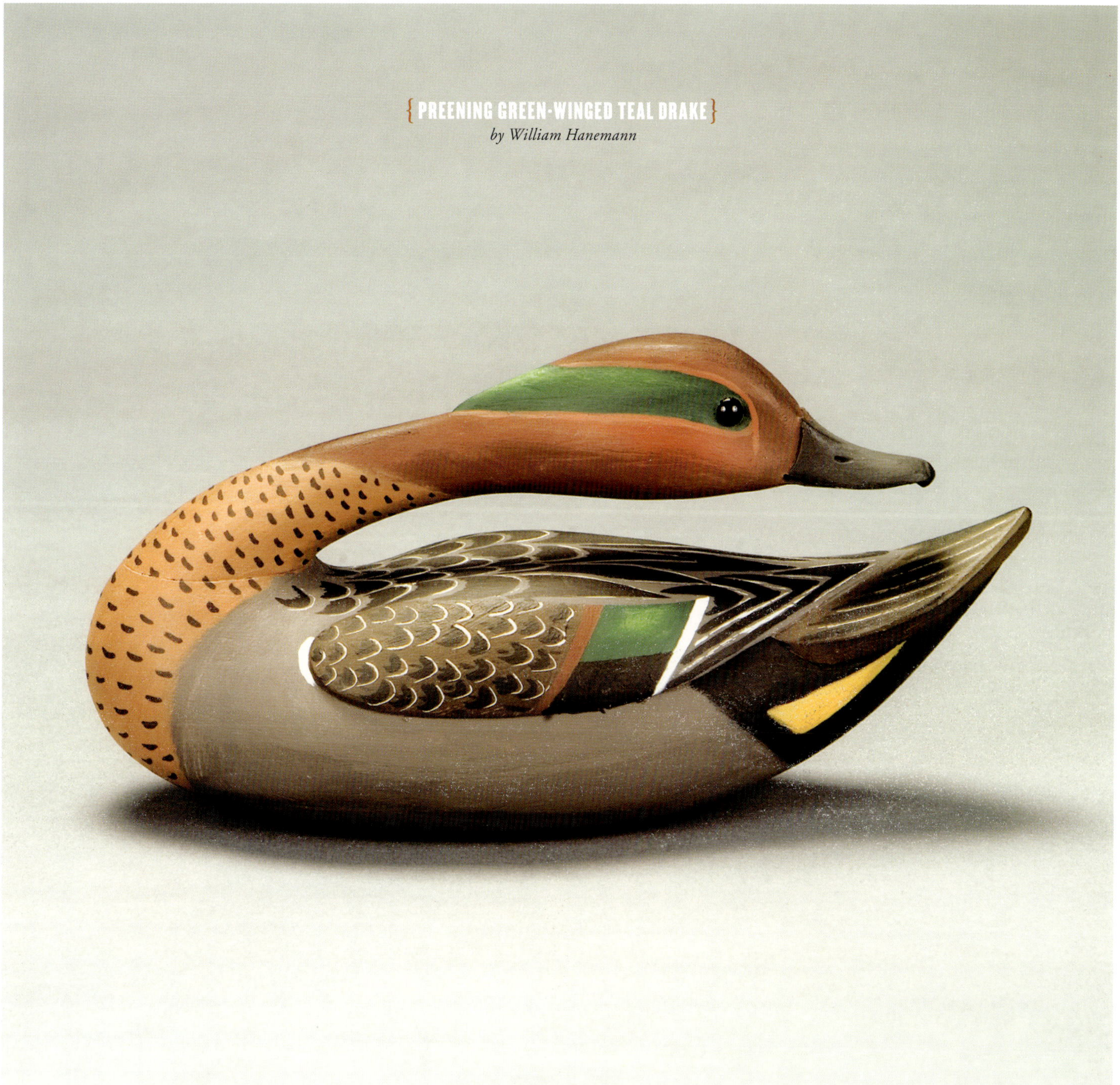

newspaper ads at $7.50 per duck. As his skills improved, he began carving intricately wrought—and expensively bought—wildfowl sculptures in the *nature morte* style. His decorative still life sculptures reflect the influence of George Viavant (1872–1925), the New Orleans painter whose works lined the walls of Hanemann's paternal grandfather's home.

Now aged 60, with more than 40 years of carving behind him, Hanemann largely eschews the high-tech tools (e.g. diamond- or ruby-tipped drills, woodburners, and airbrushing implements) used by decorative carvers in favor of more traditional methods. In his work, the art of Louisiana wildfowl carving comes full circle.

IN RECOGNITION

CHARLIE BOSCH
CHARLES W. FRANK JR.
DAVID HALL
JIMMIE HANEMANN
ROBYN HARDY, MD
KEVIN VIGUERIE
CHARLES SPENCER WOOD, MD

OVER THE COURSE OF THE LAST CENTURY, decoy carving in southeast Louisiana has evolved from a habit of necessity to a pursuit of artistic perfection. The work of Louisiana's early decoy carvers long went unacknowledged by collectors outside the region, and books such as Joel Barber's 1934 *Wild Fowl Decoys* perpetuated the belief that Louisiana, unlike the Mid-Atlantic, New England, or Great Lakes regions, had no notable carvers. It was not until the early 1950s, under the stewardship of Jimmie Hanemann, that southeast Louisiana decoys began to attract attention as discrete objects worthy of preservation and collection. Following Hanemann's lead, other individuals—writers, hunters, collectors, conservationists, and enthusiasts—began to champion the carving traditions of southeast Louisiana. Through their efforts, Louisiana decoys have gained international recognition as legitimate works of art. The Historic New Orleans Collection is honored to recognize the pioneers listed above. *Birds of a Feather: Wildfowl Carving in Southeast Louisiana* truly represents the fruits of their labors.

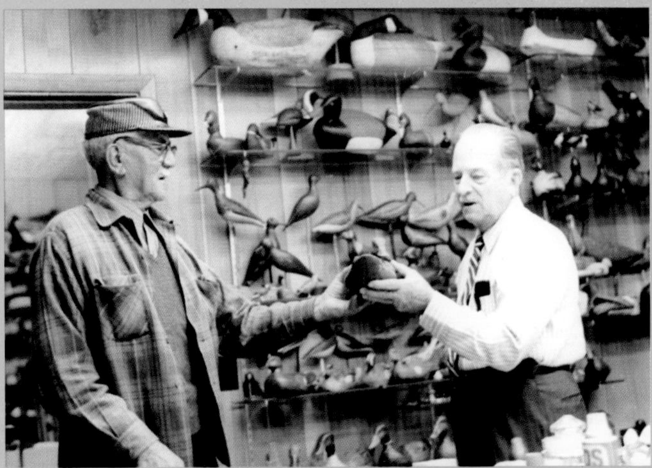

Jimmie Hanemann (right) with carver Mitchel Lafrance, from the collection of Brian Cheramie and David Hall

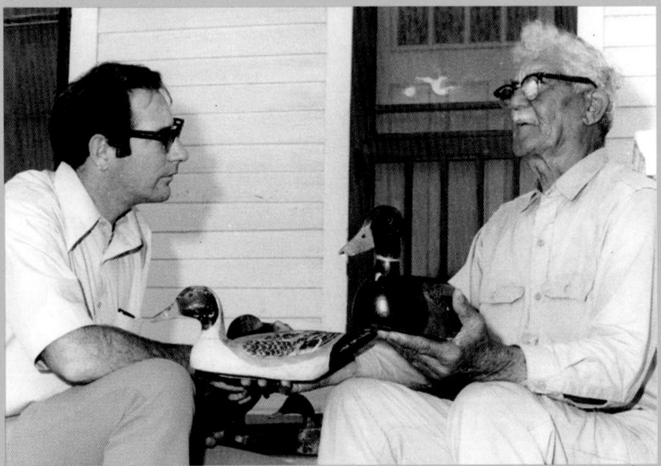

David Hall (left) with carver Mitchel Lafrance, from the collection of Brian Cheramie and David Hall

EXHIBITION CHECKLIST

{BIRDS OF A FEATHER}

Wildfowl Carving in Southeast Louisiana

PART 1

EARLY WORKING DECOYS: A NOTE ABOUT ATTRIBUTION

WORKING DECOYS *were functional objects intended for use by duck hunters. Though the occasional decoy bears the name of its maker and a date, such is hardly the norm. Collectors have done a great deal to document carvers' life dates and periods of activity. The network of family, friends, apprentices, and admirers of older-generation decoy carvers has provided information that has given structure to the historical record—including many sound attributions of a decoy's maker. In the following checklist, firm dates are given when known, extracted from sources that range from tombstones to U. S. censuses and Social Security death index records. Date ranges are based on anecdotal evidence and other less official sources. The curators welcome comments from those who can assist in refining the biographical details of Louisiana decoy carvers. Species names throughout the checklist derive from the Cornell University Lab of Ornithology's bird guide.*

HOUMA AND BAYOU TERREBONNE

MARK WHIPPLE (1884–1961)

1 **Pintail drake**
cypress root
courtesy of an anonymous lender

2 **Canvasback drake**
cypress root
courtesy of an anonymous lender

3 **Redhead drake**
cypress root
courtesy of an anonymous lender

4 **Mallard drake**
cypress root
courtesy of an anonymous lender

5 **Mallard hen**
cypress root
courtesy of an anonymous lender

6 **Mallard hen, minnow chaser**
cypress root
courtesy of an anonymous lender

7 **Blue-winged teal drake**
cypress root
courtesy of an anonymous lender

WALTON CHAMPAGNE (1880–1963)

8 **Canvasback drake**
cypress root
courtesy of an anonymous lender

9 **Mallard hen**
cypress root
courtesy of an anonymous lender

10 **Mallard drake**
cypress root
courtesy of an anonymous lender

LAURENT VERDIN SR. (1909–1991)

11 **Spoonbill drake**
cypress root
courtesy of an anonymous lender

12 **Coot**
cypress root, ca. 1930
courtesy of an anonymous lender

13 **Purple gallinule**
cypress root, ca. 1930
courtesy of an anonymous lender

14 **Coot**
cypress root, ca. 1930
courtesy of an anonymous lender

15 **Purple gallinule**
cypress root, ca. 1930
courtesy of an anonymous lender

16 **Blue-winged teal**
cypress root, ca. 1930
courtesy of an anonymous lender

17 **Blue-winged teal**
cypress root, ca. 1930
courtesy of an anonymous lender

18 **Blue-winged teal**
cypress root, ca. 1930
courtesy of an anonymous lender

UNKNOWN CARVER

19 **Mallard hen, open-billed**
cypress root
courtesy of an anonymous lender

BAYOU LAFOURCHE

REME ANGE ROUSSEL (1903–1972)

20 **Gray duck drake**
tupelo gum
courtesy of an anonymous lender

21 **Pintail drake**
tupelo gum
courtesy of an anonymous lender

22 **Mallard hen**
tupelo gum
courtesy of an anonymous lender

23 **Mallard drake**
tupelo gum
courtesy of an anonymous lender

24 **Canvasback hen**
tupelo gum
courtesy of an anonymous lender

25 **Canvasback drake**
tupelo gum
courtesy of an anonymous lender

26 **Blue-winged teal drake**
tupelo gum
courtesy of an anonymous lender

27 **Blue-winged teal hen**
tupelo gum
courtesy of an anonymous lender

28 **Ring-necked duck**
tupelo gum
gift of an anonymous donor
1976.7.8

WADE LEBLANC (CA. 1915–1990)

29 **Mallard drake**
cypress root
courtesy of an anonymous lender

XAVIER ELOI BOURG (1901–1984)

30 **Mallard drake**
cypress root
courtesy of an anonymous lender

31 **Mallard hen**
cypress root
courtesy of an anonymous lender

32 **Teal drake**
tupelo gum
gift of an anonymous donor
1976.7.4

33 **Pintail drake**
cypress root
courtesy of an anonymous lender

34 **Pintail hen**
cypress root
courtesy of an anonymous lender

RICHARD WAGUESPACK (B. 1917) & OCTAVE MONIER (1917–2000)

35 **Pintail drake**
tupelo gum
courtesy of an anonymous lender

36 **Pintail hen**
tupelo gum
courtesy of an anonymous lender

SIDNEY FORET (CA. 1902–1983)

37 **Pintail drake**
tupelo gum
courtesy of an anonymous lender

38 **Pintail hen**
tupelo gum
courtesy of an anonymous lender

THEODULE PERTUIT (1909–1974)

39 **Mallard drake**
tupelo gum
courtesy of an anonymous lender

40 **Mallard hen**
tupelo gum
courtesy of an anonymous lender

41 **Ring-necked hen**
tupelo gum
courtesy of an anonymous lender

42 **Canvasback drake**
tupelo gum
courtesy of an anonymous lender

DEWEY PERTUIT (1901–1967)

43 **Coot**
tupelo gum
gift of an anonymous donor
1976.7.12

JOSEPH J. SERIGNY (1926–1999)

44 **Blue-winged teal drake**
cypress root
courtesy of an anonymous lender

CLOVIS VIZIER (CA. 1885–1975)

45 **Blue-winged teal, preener**
cypress root
courtesy of an anonymous lender

46 **Green-winged teal, preener**
cypress root
courtesy of an anonymous lender

47 **Mallard drake**
cypress root
courtesy of an anonymous lender

48 **Mallard hen**
cypress root
courtesy of an anonymous lender

49 **Pintail drake**
cypress root
courtesy of an anonymous lender

50 **Eagle**
cypress root
on loan from the collection
of Jimmie Hanemann

ODEE VIZIER (1890–1969)

51 **Blue-winged teal drake**
cypress root
courtesy of an anonymous lender

52 **Pintail drake, minnow chaser**
cypress root
courtesy of an anonymous lender

BEAUREGARD VIZIER (1865–1934)

53 **Pintail drake**
cypress root
courtesy of an anonymous lender

attributed to NEDVILLE "PANK" MARTIN

54 **Mallard drake, pirate decoy**
cypress root
courtesy of an anonymous lender

DES ALLEMANDS AND BAYOU GAUCHE

MARC ALCIDE COMARDELLE (CA. 1890–1955)

55 **Mallard drake**
cypress root
courtesy of an anonymous lender

56 **Ring-necked drake**
cypress root
courtesy of an anonymous lender

57 **Hooded merganser drake**
cypress root
courtesy of an anonymous lender

58 **Mallard drake**
cypress root
on loan from the collection
of Jimmie Hanemann

ALBERT COMARDELLE (1889–1960)

59 **Mallard drake**
cypress root
courtesy of an anonymous lender

EDDIE GRANIER (1900–1943)

60 **Pintail drake**
cypress root
courtesy of an anonymous lender

61 **Pintail hen**
cypress root
courtesy of an anonymous lender

62 **Mallard drake**
cypress root
courtesy of an anonymous lender

63 **Ring-necked drake**
cypress root
courtesy of an anonymous lender

FRANK DUFRENE (1900–1960)

64 **Canvasback drake**
cypress root
courtesy of an anonymous lender

NEW ORLEANS

JIM MOSSMEIER (1896/7–1969)

65 **Pintail drake**
cypress root
courtesy of an anonymous lender

66 **Mallard drake**
cypress root
courtesy of an anonymous lender

67 **Mallard hen**
cypress root
courtesy of an anonymous lender

68 **Snow goose drake**
cypress root
courtesy of an anonymous lender

69 **Snow goose hen, preener**
cypress root
courtesy of an anonymous lender

70 **Blue-winged teal drake**
cypress root
courtesy of an anonymous lender

71 **Blue-winged teal hen**
cypress root
courtesy of an anonymous lender

72 **Northern shoveler drake**
cypress root
courtesy of an anonymous lender

73 **Northern shoveler hen**
cypress root
courtesy of an anonymous lender

74 **Pintail drake**
cypress root, 1949
on loan from the collection
of Jimmie Hanemann

OSCAR MURPHY (CA. 1850–1919)

75 **Green-winged teal drake**
cypress root
courtesy of an anonymous lender

76 **Ring-necked drake**
cypress root
courtesy of an anonymous lender

77 **Pintail drake**
cypress root
courtesy of an anonymous lender

78 **Blue-winged teal drake**
cypress root
courtesy of an anonymous lender

79 **Mallard drake**
cypress root
courtesy of an anonymous lender

80 **Mallard hen**
cypress root
courtesy of an anonymous lender

JOHN P. COURET (1881–1967)

81 **Pintail drake**
cypress root
courtesy of an anonymous lender

82 **Mallard hen**
cypress root
courtesy of an anonymous lender

83 **Mallard drake**
cypress root
courtesy of an anonymous lender

ROBERT F. COURET (1909–1995), Lifelike Lures

84 **Mallard hen**
balsa
courtesy of an anonymous lender

85 **Mallard drake**
balsa
courtesy of an anonymous lender

AL BEYL (1900–1957)

86 **Pintail drake**
balsa
courtesy of an anonymous lender

87 **Canvasback drake**
balsa
courtesy of an anonymous lender

88 **Ring-necked drake**
balsa
courtesy of an anonymous lender

89 **Ring-necked drake**
cypress root
on loan from the collection of Jimmie Hanemann

FRANCIS UZEE (1923–2002)

90 **Mallard drake**
cypress root
courtesy of an anonymous lender

JOHN SCOTT YOUNG (1911–1982)

91 **Mallard drake**
cypress root
courtesy of an anonymous lender

92 **Pintail drake**
balsa
courtesy of an anonymous lender

MICHAEL FRADY (1911–1994)

93 **Green-winged teal drake**
cypress root head; balsa body
courtesy of an anonymous lender

94 **Green-winged teal hen, preener**
cypress root head; balsa body
courtesy of an anonymous lender

GEORGE S. MOREL (1888–1969)

95 **Pintail drake**
cypress root
courtesy of an anonymous lender

CASSIUS PEACOCK (1887–1958)

96 **Coot**
tupelo gum
gift of an anonymous donor
1976.7.5

DAVE HYMEL (CA. 1900–1970)

97 **Pintail drake**
balsa body; cypress root head
courtesy of an anonymous lender

UNKNOWN CARVER

98 **Pintail drake**
cypress root
on loan from the collection of Jimmie Hanemann

SOUTH OF NEW ORLEANS: UPPER PLAQUEMINES

GASTON ISADORE (1871–1932)

99 **Pintail drake**
cypress root
courtesy of an anonymous lender

100 **Mallard drake**
cypress root
courtesy of an anonymous lender

101 **Mallard hen**
cypress root
courtesy of an anonymous lender

JULES FREDERICK (1870–1954)

102 **Mallard drake**
cypress root
courtesy of an anonymous lender

103 **Mallard hen**
cypress root
courtesy of an anonymous lender

attributed to MITCHEL LAFRANCE (1882–1979), GEORGE FREDERICK JR. (1907–1977), & CHARLES NUMA JOEFRAU (1913–1983)

104 **Pintail hen, preener**
cypress root
courtesy of an anonymous lender

105 **Green-winged teal drake**
cypress root
courtesy of an anonymous lender

106 **Green-winged teal hen**
cypress root
courtesy of an anonymous lender

107 **Green-winged teal drake**
cypress root
courtesy of an anonymous lender

108 **Green-winged teal hen**
cypress root
courtesy of an anonymous lender

109 **Green-winged teal hen**
cypress root
courtesy of an anonymous lender

110 **Green-winged teal drake**
cypress root
courtesy of an anonymous lender

111 **Mallard drake**
cypress root
courtesy of an anonymous lender

112 **Mallard hen**
cypress root
courtesy of an anonymous lender

113 **Mallard hen**
cypress root
courtesy of an anonymous lender

114 **Mallard drake**
cypress root, ca. 1930
on loan from the collection of Jimmie Hanemann

115 **Blue-winged teal drake**
cypress root, "early" example
on loan from the collection of Jimmie Hanemann

116 **Blue-winged teal drake**
cypress root
on loan from the collection of Jimmie Hanemann

117 **Pintail hen**
cypress root
courtesy of an anonymous lender

118 **Green-winged teal drake, preener**
cypress root
courtesy of an anonymous lender

119 **Green-winged teal hen, preener**
cypress root
courtesy of an anonymous lender

120 **Green-winged teal hen, preener**
cypress root
courtesy of an anonymous lender

121 **Pintail drake, preener**
cypress root
courtesy of an anonymous lender

122 **American black duck (black mallard)**
cypress root
courtesy of an anonymous lender

123 **Mallard hen, preener**
cypress root
courtesy of an anonymous lender

124 **Mallard drake, swimmer**
cypress root
courtesy of an anonymous lender

125 **Canvasback drake**
cypress root
courtesy of an anonymous lender

126 **Mallard hen, preener**
cypress root
courtesy of an anonymous lender

127 **Mallard drake**
cypress root
courtesy of an anonymous lender

128 **Blue-winged teal, preener**
cypress root
courtesy of an anonymous lender

ADAM ANSARDI (1885–1953)

129 **Mallard hen**
cypress root
courtesy of an anonymous lender

130 **Mallard drake**
cypress root
courtesy of an anonymous lender

131 **Pintail drake**
cypress root
courtesy of an anonymous lender

132 **Green-winged teal drake**
cypress root
courtesy of an anonymous lender

VICTOR ALFONSO (1899–1982)

133 **Mallard drake, preener**
cypress root
courtesy of an anonymous lender

MATTHEW LEITEL (1904–1968)

134 **Pintail drake**
cypress root
courtesy of an anonymous lender

135 **Blue-winged teal drake**
cypress root
courtesy of an anonymous lender

SIDNEY DUPLESSIS (1870–1950)

136 **Pintail drake**
cypress root
courtesy of an anonymous lender

137 **Mallard drake**
cypress root
courtesy of an anonymous lender

138 **Mallard hen**
cypress root
courtesy of an anonymous lender

JOHN NEVILLE DONEWAR (1883–1965)

139 **Mallard drake**
cypress root
on loan from the collection of Jimmie Hanemann

UNKNOWN CARVER

140 **Mallard drake**
cypress root
courtesy of an anonymous lender

MOUTH OF THE MISSISSIPPI RIVER: LOWER PLAQUEMINES

CHARLES ARMSTRONG (1887–1954)

141 **Mallard drake**
cypress root
courtesy of an anonymous lender

142 **Pintail drake**
cypress root
courtesy of an anonymous lender

143 **Canvasback drake**
cypress root
courtesy of an anonymous lender

144 **Green-winged teal drake, preener**
cypress root
on loan from the collection of Jimmie Hanemann

145 **Mallard drake, preener, half-sized**
cypress root, ca. 1919
on loan from the collection of Jimmie Hanemann

146 **Pintail drake**
cypress root, ca. 1918
on loan from the collection of Jimmie Hanemann

NICOLE VIDACOVICH (1853–1945)

147 **Green-winged teal drake**
cypress root
courtesy of an anonymous lender

148 **Ring-necked drake**
cypress root
courtesy of an anonymous lender

149 **Mallard drake**
cypress root
courtesy of an anonymous lender

150 **Mallard hen**
cypress root
courtesy of an anonymous lender

151 **Green-winged teal drake**
cypress root
courtesy of an anonymous lender

152 **Canvasback drake**
cypress root
courtesy of an anonymous lender

153 **Mallard drake**
cypress root
courtesy of an anonymous lender

154 **Mallard hen**
cypress root
courtesy of an anonymous lender

155 **Pintail drake**
cypress root
courtesy of an anonymous lender

HYACINTHE SCOBEL (1877–1961)

156 **Pintail hen**
cypress root
courtesy of an anonymous lender

ARTHUR JOHN DUGAR (1882–1962)

157 **Green-winged teal hen**
cypress root
courtesy of an anonymous lender

158 **Mallard hen**
cypress root
on loan from the collection of Jimmie Hanemann

EAST OF NEW ORLEANS TO SHELL BEACH

DOMINGO CAMPO (1883–1953)

159 **Gray duck drake**
cypress root
courtesy of an anonymous lender

160 **Scaup**
cypress root
courtesy of an anonymous lender

161 **Pintail drake**
cypress root
courtesy of an anonymous lender

162 **Mallard drake**
cypress root
courtesy of an anonymous lender

163 **Mallard hen**
cypress root
courtesy of an anonymous lender

164 **Widgeon drake**
cypress root
courtesy of an anonymous lender

165 **Mallard drake**
cypress root
courtesy of an anonymous lender

166 **Green-winged drake, standing preener**
cypress root
courtesy of an anonymous lender

OMAR PEREZ (1857–1951)

167 **Pintail drake**
cypress root
courtesy of an anonymous lender

168 **Mallard drake**
cypress root
courtesy of an anonymous lender

ANTONAISE ST. GERMAIN (CA. 1885–1957)

169 **Mallard hen, preener**
cypress root
courtesy of an anonymous lender

170 **Mallard drake**
cypress root
courtesy of an anonymous lender

171 **Blue-winged teal hen, preener**
cypress root
courtesy of an anonymous lender

172 **Blue-winged teal drake**
cypress root
courtesy of an anonymous lender

JAMES CURTIS ROUSSEL (1911–2007)

173 **Pintail hen**
cypress root
courtesy of an anonymous lender

174 **Pintail drake**
cypress root
courtesy of an anonymous lender

175 **Mallard drake**
cypress root
courtesy of an anonymous lender

176 **Mallard hen**
cypress root
courtesy of an anonymous lender

177 **Pintail drake**
cypress root
courtesy of an anonymous lender

DENIS PEREIRA (CA. 1894–1981)

178 **Green-winged teal hen**
cypress root, ca. 1914
courtesy of an anonymous lender

179 **Green-winged teal drake**
cypress root, ca. 1914
courtesy of an anonymous lender

UNKNOWN CARVER

180 **Gadwall drake**
cypress root
courtesy of an anonymous lender

EXHIBITION CHECKLIST

{BIRDS OF A FEATHER}

Wildfowl Carving in Southeast Louisiana

PART 2

A NOTE ABOUT CONTEMPORARY CARVINGS

UNLIKE WORKING DECOYS, *which were seldom signed or dated, decorative carvings present fewer attribution challenges. Those listed here are exemplars of the contemporary carver's art. Some of the artists represented in Part 2 of the exhibition, such as Laurent Verdin Sr., also appear in Part 1—a reminder that no firm date marks the transition from carving for use to carving for show. Some of Louisiana's finest early carvers made the occasional decorative piece. Likewise, some of today's most celebrated decorative carvers still produce birds in the "gunner" style—even though these decoys are unlikely ever to be used in the hunt. One decorative form that bridges the early period to the late is the miniature decoy, typically produced as a souvenir or keepsake.*

WILLIE BADEAUX (B. 1943)

Green-winged teal drake
tupelo gum, 2005
on loan from the collection of Willie Badeaux

Green-winged teal hen
tupelo gum, 2005
on loan from the collection of Willie Badeaux

Mallard hen
tupelo gum, 2004
on loan from the collection of Willie Badeaux

Green-winged teal drake, preener
tupelo gum, 2004
on loan from the collection of Willie Badeaux

American black duck (black mallard) drake
tupelo gum, 2003
on loan from the collection of Willie Badeaux

Canvasback drake
tupelo gum, 2003
on loan from the collection of Willie Badeaux

DICK BONNER (B. 1937)

Osprey
tupelo gum, 2006
on loan from the collection of Dick Bonner

Wood duck drake, standing
tupelo gum, 2006
on loan from the collection of Dick Bonner

American widgeon drake, floating decorative
tupelo gum, 1987
on loan from the collection of Dick Bonner

Blue-winged teal drake, preener
tupelo gum, 1987
on loan from the collection of Dick Bonner

MIKE BONNER (B. 1956)

Pintail drake
tupelo gum, 2006
on loan from the collection of Mike Bonner

Mallard drake
tupelo gum, 2007
on loan from the collection of Mike Bonner

Blue-winged teal drake
tupelo gum, 2006
on loan from the collection of Mike Bonner

Blue-winged teal hen
tupelo gum, 2006
on loan from the collection of Mike Bonner

JETT BRUNET (B. 1964)

Pintail hen
cypress root or tupelo gum, 1982
courtesy of an anonymous lender

Pintail drake
cypress root or tupelo gum, 1982
courtesy of an anonymous lender

Mallard hen
cypress root or tupelo gum, 1983
courtesy of an anonymous lender

Mallard drake
cypress root or tupelo gum, 1983
courtesy of an anonymous lender

Redhead hen
cypress root or tupelo gum, 1988
courtesy of an anonymous lender

Redhead drake
cypress root or tupelo gum, 1988
courtesy of an anonymous lender

Ruddy duck hen
cypress root or tupelo gum, 1985
courtesy of an anonymous lender

Ruddy duck drake
cypress root or tupelo gum, 1985
courtesy of an anonymous lender

Scaup hen
cypress root or tupelo gum, 1987
courtesy of an anonymous lender

Scaup drake
cypress root or tupelo gum, 1987
courtesy of an anonymous lender

American black duck (black mallard) drake
cypress root or tupelo gum, 1984
courtesy of an anonymous lender

JUDE BRUNET (B. 1969)

Ring-necked hen
cypress root or tupelo gum, 1994
courtesy of an anonymous lender

Ring-necked drake
cypress root or tupelo gum, 1994
courtesy of an anonymous lender

Gadwall hen
cypress root or tupelo gum, 1996/7
courtesy of an anonymous lender

Gadwall drake
cypress root or tupelo gum, 1996/7
courtesy of an anonymous lender

TAN BRUNET (B. 1938)

Pintail drake
cypress root or tupelo gum, 1977
courtesy of an anonymous lender

Pintail drake
cypress root or tupelo gum, 1985
courtesy of an anonymous lender

Mallard drake
cypress root or tupelo gum, 1979
courtesy of an anonymous lender

Canvasback drake
cypress root or tupelo gum, 1984
courtesy of an anonymous lender

Canvasback hen
cypress root or tupelo gum, 1984
courtesy of an anonymous lender

Green-winged teal hen
cypress root or tupelo gum, 1982
courtesy of an anonymous lender

Green-winged teal drake
cypress root or tupelo gum, 1982
courtesy of an anonymous lender

Redhead hen
cypress root or tupelo gum, 1983
courtesy of an anonymous lender

Redhead drake
cypress root or tupelo gum, 1983
courtesy of an anonymous lender

Pintail hen
cypress root or tupelo gum, 1985
courtesy of an anonymous lender

Mallard hen
cypress root or tupelo gum, 1983
courtesy of an anonymous lender

Widgeon hen
cypress root or tupelo gum, 1988
courtesy of an anonymous lender

Widgeon drake
cypress root or tupelo gum, 1988
courtesy of an anonymous lender

Wood duck drake
cypress root or tupelo gum, 1980
courtesy of an anonymous lender

Wood duck hen
cypress root or tupelo gum, 1986
courtesy of an anonymous lender

Red-breasted merganser drake
cypress root or tupelo gum, 1985
courtesy of an anonymous lender

Cackling goose
cypress root or tupelo gum, 1990
courtesy of an anonymous lender

Blue-winged teal hen
cypress root or tupelo gum, 1983
courtesy of an anonymous lender

Blue-winged teal drake
cypress root or tupelo gum, 1988
courtesy of an anonymous lender

JAMIE DEMPSTER

"Old squaw" drake
cypress root or tupelo gum
courtesy of an anonymous lender

LANDRY DEMPSTER

Decoy head and body profile
cypress root or tupelo gum, 1975
courtesy of an anonymous lender

Decoy head and body profile
cypress root or tupelo gum, 1975
courtesy of an anonymous lender

LANDRY DEMPSTER & JAMIE DEMPSTER

Pair of wood ducks on driftwood
cypress root or tupelo gum, 1975–1977
courtesy of an anonymous lender

DAVID HALL

Green-winged teal hen
cypress root, 1973
on loan from the collection of Jimmie Hanemann

WILLIAM HANEMANN (B. 1947)

Pintail drake, preener
cypress root
courtesy of an anonymous lender

Green-winged teal drake, preener
cypress root
courtesy of an anonymous lender

Green-winged teal hen, preener
cypress root
courtesy of an anonymous lender

Eastern wild turkey
tupelo, mahogany, ivory, oil paint
courtesy of an anonymous lender

CHARLES HUTCHISON (1921–1995)

Mallard hen
tupelo gum or cypress root, ca. 1980
on loan from the collection of Charlotte Hoggatt

Mallard drake
tupelo gum or cypress root, ca. 1980
on loan from the collection of Charlotte Hoggatt

CAL KINGSMILL (B. 1948)

Mallard drake
cypress root or tupelo gum, 1985
on loan from the collection of Cal Kingsmill

Mallard hen
cypress root or tupelo gum, 1985
on loan from the collection of Cal Kingsmill

Spoonbill drake
cypress root or tupelo gum, 2005
on loan from the collection of Cal Kingsmill

Spoonbill hen
cypress root or tupelo gum, 2005
on loan from the collection of Cal Kingsmill

Pintail hen
cypress root or tupelo gum, 1985
on loan from the collection of Cal Kingsmill

Pintail drake
cypress root or tupelo gum, 1985
on loan from the collection of Cal Kingsmill

RUSSELL MARTIN SR.

Gadwall hen
cypress root or tupelo gum, ca. 1975
courtesy of an anonymous lender

Gadwall drake
cypress root or tupelo gum, ca. 1975
courtesy of an anonymous lender

Redhead hen
cypress root or tupelo gum, 1975
courtesy of an anonymous lender

Redhead drake
cypress root or tupelo gum, ca. 1975
courtesy of an anonymous lender

Widgeon hen
cypress root or tupelo gum, ca. 1975
courtesy of an anonymous lender

Widgeon drake
cypress root or tupelo gum
courtesy of an anonymous lender

Blue-winged teal hen
cypress root or tupelo gum, ca. 1975
courtesy of an anonymous lender

Blue-winged teal drake
cypress root or tupelo gum, ca. 1975
courtesy of an anonymous lender

Pintail hen
cypress root or tupelo gum, ca. 1975
courtesy of an anonymous lender

Pintail drake
cypress root or tupelo gum, ca. 1975
courtesy of an anonymous lender

Mallard hen
cypress root or tupelo gum, ca. 1975
courtesy of an anonymous lender

Mallard drake
cypress root or tupelo gum, ca. 1975
courtesy of an anonymous lender

Green-winged teal hen
cypress root or tupelo gum, ca. 1975
courtesy of an anonymous lender

Green-winged teal drake
cypress root or tupelo gum, ca. 1975
courtesy of an anonymous lender

Wood duck hen
cypress root or tupelo gum, 1975
courtesy of an anonymous lender

Wood duck drake
cypress root or tupelo gum, 1975
courtesy of an anonymous lender

Wood duck hen
cypress root or tupelo gum, 1975
courtesy of an anonymous lender

Wood duck drake
cypress root or tupelo gum, 1975
courtesy of an anonymous lender

Pintail drake, oversized
cypress root or tupelo gum
courtesy of an anonymous lender

RICHARD REEVES

Great horned owl with bobwhite quail
tupelo gum, 2006
on loan from the collection of Richard Reeves

Canada goose
tupelo gum, 1994
on loan from the collection of Richard Reeves

Mallard hen
tupelo gum, 2003
on loan from the collection of Richard Reeves

Wood duck drake
tupelo gum, 2006
on loan from the collection of Richard Reeves

LAURENT VERDIN SR. (1909–1991)

White pelican, standing
cypress root or tupelo gum
courtesy of an anonymous lender

Spoonbill
cypress root or tupelo gum
courtesy of an anonymous lender

Spoonbill drake
cypress root or tupelo gum, ca. 1960-1970
courtesy of an anonymous lender

Mallard hen
cypress root or tupelo gum, ca. 1960-1970
courtesy of an anonymous lender

Mallard drake
cypress root or tupelo gum, ca. 1960-1970
courtesy of an anonymous lender

Gadwall hen, head turned
cypress root or tupelo gum
courtesy of an anonymous lender

Gadwall drake, head turned
cypress root or tupelo gum
courtesy of an anonymous lender

Pintail hen
cypress root or tupelo gum
courtesy of an anonymous lender

Pintail drake
cypress root or tupelo gum
courtesy of an anonymous lender

Marsh hen, standing
cypress root or tupelo gum
courtesy of an anonymous lender

American black duck (black mallard) hen, head turned
cypress root or tupelo gum
courtesy of an anonymous lender

American black duck (black mallard) hen
cypress root or tupelo gum
courtesy of an anonymous lender

American black duck (black mallard) drake
cypress root or tupelo gum
courtesy of an anonymous lender

Green-winged teal hen
cypress root or tupelo gum
courtesy of an anonymous lender

Green-winged teal drake
cypress root or tupelo gum
courtesy of an anonymous lender

Green-winged teal hen
cypress root or tupelo gum
courtesy of an anonymous lender

LAURENT VERDIN JR. (B. 1936)

Mallard hen
cypress root or tupelo gum
courtesy of an anonymous lender

Mallard drake
cypress root or tupelo gum
courtesy of an anonymous lender

Pintail hen
cypress root or tupelo gum
courtesy of an anonymous lender

Pintail drake
cypress root or tupelo gum
courtesy of an anonymous lender

Blue-winged teal hen
cypress root or tupelo gum
courtesy of an anonymous lender

Blue-winged teal drake
cypress root or tupelo gum
courtesy of an anonymous lender

Green-winged teal hen
cypress root or tupelo gum
courtesy of an anonymous lender

Green-winged teal drake
cypress root or tupelo gum
courtesy of an anonymous lender

Brown pelican
cypress root or tupelo gum
courtesy of an anonymous lender

Brown pelican
cypress root or tupelo gum
courtesy of an anonymous lender

Brown pelican
cypress root or tupelo gum
courtesy of an anonymous lender

Eagle
cypress root or tupelo gum
courtesy of an anonymous lender

Great horned owl
cypress root or tupelo gum
courtesy of an anonymous lender

Canada goose
cypress root or tupelo gum
courtesy of an anonymous lender

Gadwall hen
cypress root or tupelo gum
courtesy of an anonymous lender

Gadwall drake
cypress root or tupelo gum
courtesy of an anonymous lender

American black duck (black mallard) hen
cypress root or tupelo gum
courtesy of an anonymous lender

American black duck (black mallard) drake
cypress root or tupelo gum
courtesy of an anonymous lender

American black duck (black mallard) hen
cypress root or tupelo gum
courtesy of an anonymous lender

American black duck (black mallard) drake
cypress root or tupelo gum
courtesy of an anonymous lender

Spoonbill hen
cypress root or tupelo gum
courtesy of an anonymous lender

Spoonbill drake
cypress root or tupelo gum
courtesy of an anonymous lender

Rocking-neck spoonbill drake
cypress root or tupelo gum
courtesy of an anonymous lender

Wood duck drake
cypress root or tupelo gum
courtesy of an anonymous lender

Egret, standing
cypress root or tupelo gum
courtesy of an anonymous lender

Blue heron, standing
cypress root or tupelo gum
courtesy of an anonymous lender

Greater white-fronted goose, preener
cypress root or tupelo gum
courtesy of an anonymous lender

Pintail drake, hanging
cypress root or tupelo gum
courtesy of an anonymous lender

Rooster
cypress root or tupelo gum
courtesy of an anonymous lender

Brown pelican
cypress root or tupelo gum
courtesy of an anonymous lender

Brown pelican
cypress root or tupelo gum
courtesy of an anonymous lender

JIMMIE VIZIER (B. 1933)

American black duck (black mallard) hen
cypress root or tupelo gum, 1989
courtesy of an anonymous lender

American black duck (black mallard) drake
cypress root or tupelo gum, 1989
courtesy of an anonymous lender

Pintail hen
cypress root or tupelo gum, 1989
courtesy of an anonymous lender

Pintail drake
cypress root or tupelo gum, 1989
courtesy of an anonymous lender

Mallard hen
cypress root or tupelo gum, 1990
courtesy of an anonymous lender

Mallard drake
cypress root or tupelo gum, 1990
courtesy of an anonymous lender

Greater white-fronted goose
cypress root or tupelo gum, 1997
courtesy of an anonymous lender

Wood duck hen
tupelo gum, 2007
courtesy of an anonymous lender

Wood duck drake
tupelo gum, 2007
courtesy of an anonymous lender

American black duck (black mallard) hen
tupelo gum, ca. 1981
on loan from the collection of Jimmie Vizier

American black duck (black mallard) drake
tupelo gum, ca. 1981
on loan from the collection of Jimmie Vizier

Canada goose
tupelo gum, ca. 1985
on loan from the collection of Jimmie Vizier

Canada goose
tupelo gum, ca. 1985
on loan from the collection of Jimmie Vizier

MINIATURES BY LAURENT VERDIN SR.

Mallard hen
cypress root or tupelo gum
courtesy of an anonymous lender

Mallard drake
cypress root or tupelo gum
courtesy of an anonymous lender

Pintail hen
cypress root or tupelo gum
courtesy of an anonymous lender

Pintail drake
cypress root or tupelo gum
courtesy of an anonymous lender

Spoonbill hen
cypress root or tupelo gum
courtesy of an anonymous lender

Spoonbill drake
cypress root or tupelo gum
courtesy of an anonymous lender

Blue-winged teal hen
cypress root or tupelo gum
courtesy of an anonymous lender

Blue-winged teal drake
cypress root or tupelo gum
courtesy of an anonymous lender

Green-winged teal hen
cypress root or tupelo gum
courtesy of an anonymous lender

Green-winged teal drake
cypress root or tupelo gum
courtesy of an anonymous lender

White pelican
cypress root or tupelo gum
courtesy of an anonymous lender

White pelican
cypress root or tupelo gum
courtesy of an anonymous lender

Exhibition Curator
John H. Lawrence

Exhibition Editor
Erin Greenwald

Exhibition Coordinator
Warren J. Woods

Catalogue Photography
Keely Merritt

Exhibition Graphics
Steve Sweet

Exhibition Design
Terry Weldon
Scott Ratterree
Mitchell Long
Douglas Stallmer

Exhibition Staff
Viola Berman
Jan White Brantley
Teresa Devlin
Jessica Dorman
Larry Falgoust
Maclyn Hickey
Anna Hilderbrandt
Teresa Kirkland
Goldie Lanaux
Anne McCall
Mary Mees
Rebecca Smith
Jude Solomon
Sally Stassi

Catalogue Design
Alison Cody

Photographs, paintings, maps, and an assortment of carvers' and hunters' paraphernalia enhance the environment of *Birds of a Feather*. These items, along with the carvings identified in the exhibition checklist, bring the installation to life. The Historic New Orleans Collection gratefully acknowledges **Willie Badeaux, Dick Bonner, Mike Bonner, the photographic collection of Brian Cheramie and David Hall, the collection of Jimmie Hanemann, Charlotte Hoggatt, Cal Kingsmill, James E. Kurzweg, Richard Reeves, Jimmie Vizier, John L. Weimer** and the many anonymous lenders whose generosity made this exhibition possible.